C0-AUG-264

C'est toujours l'âme qui gagne les combats décisifs.

Jean Raspail

Reinventing Aristocracy: The Constitutional Reformation of Corporate Governance

ANDREW FRASER

Ashgate
DARTMOUTH

Aldershot • Brookfield USA • Singapore • Sydney

© Andrew Fraser 1998

All rights reserved. No part of this publication may be reproduced, stored in a retrieval system, or transmitted in any form or by any means, electronic, mechanical, photocopying, recording or otherwise without the prior permission of the publisher.

Published by
Dartmouth Publishing Company Limited
Ashgate Publishing Ltd
Gower House
Croft Road
Aldershot
Hants GU11 3HR
England

Ashgate Publishing Company
Old Post Road
Brookfield
Vermont 05036
USA

British Library Cataloguing in Publication Data
Fraser, Andrew
 Reinventing aristocracy : the constitutional reformation of
 corporate governance. - (Socio-legal studies)
 1. Corporate governance - Philosophy 2. Corporate law
 3. Aristocracy (Political science) 4. Leadership - Philosophy
 I. Title
 658.4'001

Library of Congress Cataloging-in-Publication Data
Fraser, Andrew W., 1943-
 Reinventing aristocracy : the constitutional reformation of
 corporate governance / Andrew Fraser.
   p.   cm.
 "Socio-legal series."
 Includes index.
 ISBN 1-84014-061-5 (hardbound)
 1. Corporate governance. 2. Democracy. 3. Aristocracy (Political
 science)   I. Title.
 HD2741.F73   1998   97-39115
 658.4--dc21   CIP

ISBN 1 84014 061 5

Printed and bound in Great Britain by
Creative Print and Design (Wales), Ebbw Vale

Contents

Preface

When I first studied corporate law, I was startled to find the fossilized remnants of a body politic lying at the heart of the modern business corporation. Although I had read modern history and political theory for many years and was receptive to radical critiques of the capitalist system, questions of corporate governance had never before caught my attention. Since those law school days, I have been unable to get that curious image of the corporation as a little republic out of my mind. That is not because my corporate law professor had suggested, much less insisted upon the analogy. Neither he nor my fellow students would have been much interested in a comparison of shareholders meetings and voting rights to the civic rituals of the Athenian *polis*. It seemed obvious that corporate law belonged to the world of commerce and economics and not to the realm of politics and government. Shareholders were passive investors, not active citizens.

Such assumptions still govern the teaching of corporate law throughout the common law world. Constitutional jurisprudence has followed suit. The subject of corporate governance has no place in the teaching of constitutional law. Constitutional lawyers concern themselves only with the norms governing the internal political order of the state and its relations with citizens and subjects. Working within the confines of the legal academy, it has taken a long time to develop a sustained analysis and rational argument out of a fleeting classroom intuition. But the world has changed over the past quarter century. The constitutional reformation of the corporate sector may be an idea whose time has come. Formal recognition of the corporation as a civil body politic now offers feasible solutions to many of the distinctive problems associated with what sociologists call 'reflexive modernity' and the 'risk society'.

The idea of the corporation as a civil body politic dates from an era when the classical republican tradition was still taken seriously as a guide to political practice. Corporations were constituted bodies like the aristocratic and ecclesiastical estates built into a mixed and balanced constitution. The classical conception of a constitutional balance between the one, the few and the many has been all but lost to the present generation. An undergraduate course in political theory left me puzzled by the offhand manner in which the ancient ideal of mixed government was dismissed as a defunct ideology. Inspired by the work of Hannah Arendt, I later came to see corporate bodies politic as a medium for the reconstitution of an aristocratic element in the governance of modern civil societies.

Unfortunately, aristocracy now conjures up the nasty spectre of an oppressive ruling class set over and above the common herd. Everyone, Left and Right, agrees that ruling classes are a bad thing. On the Right, this poses no problem since the impersonal meritocracy of the corporate system is said to have replaced the hereditary ruling classes of premodern times. Modernity has become more or less synonymous with democratic capitalism. The separation of investor ownership and managerial control has become a trump card in the ideological defence of the corporate system. Nevertheless much effort on the Left has been poured into an effort to pierce the corporate veil so as to unmask the face of domination. That enterprise has been to no avail since, more than ever before, the global economy has become a disembodied force of nature, if not the voice of God.

In these circumstances, a ruling class prepared to accept responsibility for the fate of the common world in which we live would come as a welcome relief. Political, economic and intellectual elites throughout the English-speaking world are suffering from a colossal failure of nerve. The ideology of democratic capitalism requires them to deny their own corporate existence while renouncing any special claim to civic authority. There has also been a failure of political imagination. The American critical legal studies movement was, for a time, a spirited intellectual revolt against liberal legalism. It fizzled out because it could not imagine alternatives to the spectacular corporate system of permanent innovation. Instead, it became mired in the divisive, dead-end politics of race and gender, thereby deepening the crisis of confidence among legal elites in every other Anglo-American society from the United Kingdom to the Antipodes.

The threatened obsolescence of the nation-state in the face of globalisation exposes the despotic potential inherent in the transnational corporate system. No one expects corporate loyalty to the states providing big business with legal personality and political protection. If the core cultures of Western civilisation are not to be sacrificed on the altar of economic growth, the corporate sector must be embedded in a coherent and binding sense of civic purpose. Given the transnational character of modern capitalism, that civilising mission must fall to the Anglo-American elites sprung from the peoples of the several nations created out of the British diaspora. Yet one cannot be confident that our best and brightest are ready, willing or able to discharge that responsibility. What, then, is to be done?

Acknowledgements

I am very grateful to a number of people who helped to clarify the ideas in this book and who through their comments and criticism encouraged its completion.

Valerie Kerruish and Wojciech Sadurski got me started and kept me going through seminars at Macquarie and Sydney law schools, respectively. John Gava, Frank Carrigan, Kathe Boehringer and Scott Veitch read and made helpful comments on several drafts. Paul Gottfried and Alan Hunt forced me to rethink aspects of the argument. Special thanks are due to my brother, Rod Fraser. He subjected the manuscript to painstaking and often scathing criticism on matters of both style and substance. He will recognise his influence on the finished work. David Campbell saw the remaining gaps in the argument and pointed me in the right direction on several vital issues. The final shape of the book owes much to his suggestions. Maggie Liston and Susan Wards created the text out of my difficult handwriting, bearing innumerable revisions with patience and good humour.

1 Aristocracy and Democracy in the Era of Reflexive Modernisation

Introduction

The argument of this book is easily summarised. To govern the business corporation in a manner appropriate to the civil constitution of a modern republican society, we will have to reinvent the theory and practice of aristocracy, aristocracy being a metaphor for the civic virtues that a free people might expect of their leaders in politics, business and intellectual life. This proposition is bound to be a tough sell in commercial societies where private wealth carries few, if any, public responsibilities. Nowadays, appeals to the noble instincts of the rich and the powerful defy common sense. *Noblesse oblige*, it seems, belongs to a world we have lost forever. To political realists and economic determinists, the past is dead and buried; markets and polls define the limits to political imagination. When invention becomes synonymous with the relentless search for novelty, aristocracy, like royalty, turns into an apparently archaic constitutional form.

Representative democracy has relegated both the aristocratic principle and hereditary kingship to the dustbin of history (the Ukanian survival of the monarchy and the House of Lords notwithstanding).[1] Almost every regime the world over now claims to be democratic. That being so, the reinvention of aristocracy must seem about as 'progressive' or 'politically relevant' to the constitution of a modern republic as the restoration of the Bourbons. Both monarchy and aristocracy are teetering on the edge of constitutional extinction. One cannot simply will them back into existence. Despite the divisions between politicians and the people, there seems to be no alternative to the democratic legitimation of power. Attempting to breathe new life into the cold constitutional corpse of aristocracy so as to set the modern body politic into motion may seem quixotic. In fact, we desperately need new forms of public life to replace those losing their vitality. In every modern society, the participation of the people in public life seems much less

1

effective now that power is slipping away from the state into the corporate sector. There, the rule of the many has been supplanted by the power of the few. The question is whether corporate elites could become the modern counterpart of the aristocratic element in earlier republican constitutions uniting the one, the few and the many.

On the surface, the notion of a reinvented aristocracy has no obvious relevance to the governance of the modern business corporation. For the corporate rich, aristocratic virtue is merely a matter of tasteful consumption. It has no application to the organised power wielded by the high and mighty. Managers and capitalists may often live like kings and even rule vast empires but they make unlikely aristocrats. The civic virtues seem altogether out of place in a corporate jungle where human nature becomes a synonym for boundless greed. As greed is (almost) always good, pandering to it has become big business. Aristocracies traditionally claimed to embody the rule of the best. What could that mean to the modern business corporation apart from another banal managerial prescription for a better than average bottom line? The answer becomes apparent only when we recognise corporate power as a vital element in the operating constitution of every modern government.

That power must be civilised. The internal governance of many private business corporations must become part of the 'civil constitution' of a modern republic. Since that term has no official status in contemporary constitutional law it requires explanation. It also needs to be rescued from its origins in an act of revolutionary hubris. In the history of the French Revolution, the idea of a civil constitution is associated with the worst excesses of Jacobin anticlericalism. The *Civil Constitution of the Clergy* adopted by the Constituent Assembly on 12 July 1790 incorporated the ecclesiastical realm into the internal political order of the revolutionary nation-state. This nationalisation of the clergy was but one of the constitutional crimes associated with the birth of the first French republic.[2] Christians were outraged as the spiritual autonomy of the Church was subordinated to the legitimation and financial needs of a bankrupt and godless revolutionary regime. Born-again free marketeers may reject the civil constitution of corporate power as yet another socialist assault on private property rights. But civilising capitalism is not a matter of subordinating the corporate economy to the state. The goal is not to displace the owners of corporate property. Indeed, the problem we face is the appropriation of public power by the corporate sector. Restoring the civic significance of share ownership is a responsible alternative to a global system of interlocking corporate fiefdoms now draining governmental power from the liberal democratic nation-state.

Corporations have constitutions. They also exercise sweeping powers of social control and economic regulation. Nevertheless the conventional wisdom tells us that corporations are legal fictions or economic entities serving business interests, not political units of government. Their powers are commonly understood as *private* or *social,* not *civil* or *public* in character. Economists, commercial lawyers and organisational sociologists have staked out prior claims to the internal order of the business corporation, leaving constitutional jurists and political scientists with little to say on the subject of corporate governance. The adjective 'civil' denotes the domain of the public-spirited *citizen* but the corporate economy is now unquestionably the realm where the self-interested *bourgeois* reigns supreme. Bourgeois hegemony is underwritten by the one share, one vote rule in corporate governance. Within the civil constitution of the corporate sector, a republican rule of one voice, one vote could apply to shareholder senates composed of active investors with a substantial stake in their joint enterprise. That procedural reform would have a profound effect on the operating constitution of the corporate welfare state. It would change the culture of business by providing public spaces for the best citizens within the corporate bourgeoisie. Given the risks imposed on us by the globalising forces of capitalist development, it is more important than ever to civilise corporate governance. Early modern republicans managed to civilise the state while leaving society to look after itself. As presently constituted, corporate capitalism may well serve the private interests of the managerial and professional classes. The public interests they share with the rest of us are less well served. No matter how well the economy performs, our control over its social, cultural and ecological consequences seems increasingly shaky and uncertain. In our darker moments, descent into high-tech barbarism seems a plausible scenario. Fortunately, members of the corporate bourgeoisie are citizens too. They possess moral as well as financial resources that could and should be brought to bear in corporate decision-making.

The constitutional law of corporate governance should aim at stimulating deliberation. This can be done by organising an orderly social conflict between the citizen and the bourgeois. That confrontation will take place not between classes but within the consciences of individuals and groups. By causing the bourgeois investor to take on the role of the citizen, the corporate constitution could open up an 'inner conflict' between what 'individuals experience as their more desirable and less desirable desires'.[3] We should not take it for granted that the preferences of citizens and investors are somehow preordained and immutable. In a modern republican society, preferences should be learned through experience, not given *a priori*.

But that seemingly innocuous reference to 'a modern republican society' conceals another problem.   Hannah Arendt claimed that modern society has fused the once separate spheres of public and private life into a vast nation-wide administration of housekeeping.   In the ancient world, women and slaves were given the task of feeding, clothing and sheltering the household.   Those who shared the public world could be free because they were no longer subject to the rule of necessity.   In modern society, the economy rules politics, not the other way around.   It follows that 'the social' has made us all slaves to economic necessity.[4]   Men once rose out of the private household to participate in the public life of the *polis*.   Modern mass societies offer individuals few public spaces in which they might *act* as citizens and *be* republicans.   This has led to the moral de-skilling of the citizenry.[5]   For Arendt, the promise of a modern 'republican society' has been undermined by the invasion of the public sphere by private economic interests.   The rise of the social marks the end of classical politics.   Modern society shrinks rather than expands the scope of the republican freedoms she hoped, somehow, to recover.   But that 'socialising process' may be reversible.   The ostensibly private sphere of corporate governance could be opened up to problems of common or public interest.   A political tradition born in the ancient city-state can bear new fruit in the modern corporate state.

Those less enamoured of the ancients view classical republican traditions as the permanent antithesis of constitutional modernity.   Modern republicanism was pioneered in the Western nation-states born in the democratic revolution of the late eighteenth century.[6]   In the name of the modern demos, the ancient institution of hereditary kingship was abolished both in France and in most of British North America.   It was not long before the traditional constitutional role of the classical few also faced extinction.   The liberties prized by the moderns have little in common with those celebrated by the ancients.   Those Australians, for example, who want to abolish the British monarchy renounce the historical legacy of the *republica Anglorum* conceived in Aristotelean terms as a stable constitutional balance between the one, the few and the many.   Instead, they portray the repudiation of our ancestral allegiance to the Crown as the constitutional corollary of sovereign nationhood.   As a 'merely symbolic' change in the corporate image of the Australian government, the creation of a republic has become an exercise in the top-down politics of state-building.[7]

For the official champions of the republican cause in Australia (and New Zealand), the identity of the nation is no longer grounded in the distinctive *nomos* of a world-wide British diaspora.   In the late eighteenth century, French and American republicans set hereditary monarchy in opposition to the general will of the nation. Today, the last ditch effort by monarchists to distinguish the Queen of Australia from the Queen of the United Kingdom simply encourages the Australian people to forget their own stake in rights and liberties once rooted in the ancient British constitution. Once held by all free-born British subjects as a form of property, an inheritance passed on from one generation to the next, the ancient constitution is to be nationalised and purged of foreign elements. Even ministers of the Crown now feel free to dismiss the British connection as a tacky and anachronistic embarrassment in their campaign to market a brand new multicultural Australia in the capitals and boardrooms of Asia. Certainly the existence of the monarchy is not perceived as a threat to the liberal or the democratic much less the bourgeois character of the Australian constitutional order. Popular sovereignty is officially proclaimed and judicially recognised as an already accomplished political reality, not as a far-distant goal.[8] At the same time, everyone understands that the people delegate their sovereignty to the state in perpetuity. As we will see, governmental power then devolves very largely into the corporate sector. Nevertheless, formal law-making authority remains vested exclusively in the legislative, judicial, executive and administrative arms of the democratic nation-state.

The question posed here is whether parliamentary democracy can and should muster the political will to lay down a new law of corporate governance so as to civilise the constitution of modern republican societies? Minimalist republicans maintain that the proclamation of a republic in an old settler dominion requires little or no positive change to existing constitutional arrangements. Utterly indifferent to the classical republican tradition, those whose only aim is to shed the British monarchy have no interest in redesigning contemporary constitutional arrangements to create a new federal distribution of authority in the corporate sector. Certainly the reinvention of aristocracy has no place on their agenda. In the classical tradition, the mixed polity had a place, not just for democracy, but for kings and nobles as well.[9] But no home-grown aristocracy ever managed to secure a foothold within the colonial constitutional order.[10] As governments throughout the Empire divided British subjects into citizens of Australia, Canada and New Zealand, both populist nationalism and official multiculturalism have worn away all but the last royal links to the ancient British constitution. Under the officially sponsored model of republicanism from above, the Queen will soon be replaced with local heads of state. To avoid any upsets, this constitutional figurehead will be selected by an entrenched parliamentary oligarchy determined to secure its own place as the seat of sovereign authority. Now being marketed as a cosmetic change in the internal political order of the

Australian nation-state, this regal republicanism aims to minimise the scope of constitutional change.

But, due to its monumental indifference to the classical tradition, minimalist republicanism is itself a contradiction in terms. The British monarchy is to be abolished by a sovereign parliament in the name of a sovereign people. Minimalists pretend that the constitution balances the legal authority of parliament by the political power of the electorate. That is to say, the conventional norms of representative democracy will endow the absolute legal sovereignty vested in the Crown in and out of Parliament with political legitimacy.[11]   But this formula cannot guarantee constitutional government once corporate power rivals that of the state.

Parliamentary politics is all too obviously beholden to moneyed interests. One need not steep oneself in the works of Aristotle, Machiavelli or Harrington to see the cynicism and mutual contempt already governing relations between the parliamentary few and the many whose constitutional role is limited to periodically choosing, in silence and secrecy, between a limited range of predigested electoral options. In fact, the ostensibly democratic rejection of both the aristocratic principle and the ancient institution of hereditary kingship simply disguises the covert reconstitution of novel forms of oligarchy and despotism within the internal political order of the modern corporate welfare state. The successful democratic assault on aristocratic privilege and the divine right of kings has not in fact prevented the emergence of ruling elites, all well served by the parliamentary regime; nor has it eliminated the corporate barons presiding over the refeudalisation of modern civil society. While many judges and all politicians kneel in public before the imaginary sovereignty of the people, corporate and professional elites routinely exercise many governmental powers as a matter of private right. Governing the institutional life of modern civil society without any apparent constitutional warrant, modern elites have come to exhibit many of the vices and few of the virtues once associated with noble orders in a mixed polity. Even in the United States, the natural aristocracy of the early republic has long since been supplanted by a managerial overclass. The principle of popular sovereignty now serves as a legal fiction disguising the de facto power of the corporate sector.

The Revolt of the Elites

It was once held by many historians that the American Revolution was a rather conservative affair, severing the constitutional link with Great Britain but doing little to upset established social and political hierarchies in the newly independent and confederated states.[12]   Gordon Wood has recently launched a major assault on that received interpretation of the revolutionary experience in America. He demonstrates that the revolution transformed American society radically and irrevocably by extending the principle of equality into every aspect of public life. Since every branch of government and public administration owed its existence to the people, there was no constitutional room for kings or aristocrats. For fifty or more years after the Declaration of Independence, 'common ordinary men stripped the northern gentry of their pretensions, charged them at every turn with being fakes and shams, and relentlessly undermined their capacity to rule'. By destroying the last trace of aristocracy in the American constitutional order, democrats 'transformed what it meant to be a gentleman and a political leader in America'.[13]

Leisured independence ceased abruptly to be either a desirable way of life for the propertied classes or a qualification for the exercise of public authority. Property lost its formal constitutional significance and fell instead under the rubric of private law. Wood emphasises the radical character of this transformation but there is a sense in which the radical democratic attack on monarchy and aristocracy in America amounted to a sort of political shadow boxing. As the legal history of the American corporation reveals all too clearly, moneyed interests were more than willing to abandon the notion that property ownership should carry with it the sort of public responsibility and civic obligation associated with the aristocratic ideal of *noblesse oblige*. The public burdens of property ownership came to count for much less than the private benefits it conferred, nowhere more obviously than in the realm of corporate governance.

Share ownership became a means of systematically negating the civic significance of property ownership. Before American independence, property was the material basis for the participation of landowners in the political nation. No one doubted that owners were responsible for the uses to which their property was put.   Sheltering behind the veil of incorporation, shareholders relinquish political responsibility for corporate behaviour while shielding themselves from financial liability as well. The share came to be valued, not for the *membership* it conferred in a corporate body politic, but rather for the *ownership* of a valuable economic and financial asset. Wood suggests that no American revolutionary could have predicted that equality would mean, 'not just that a man was as good as his neighbour and possessed equal rights' but also that he would be 'weighed by his purse, not by his mind, and according to the preponderance of that, he rises or sinks in the scale of individual opinion'. It remained axiomatic that the democratic norm of equality admitted of no formal superiority in the public realm. Radical democrats continued to assert that 'no man has a greater claim of special privilege for his £100,000 than I have for my £5'.[14] But within the 'private' realm of corporate governance, public opinion gave free rein to the prestige and power of wealth. Before long, the voice of a shareholder with one hundred or one million shares would carry one hundred or one million times the weight of a member holding but one share in a common corporate enterprise. Not surprisingly, wealthy investors soon became quite comfortable with that interpretation of democratic equality. Nowadays, as a consequence, the wealthy are not at all eager to reconstitute themselves as a natural aristocracy with a special constitutional responsibility for the welfare of the community at large.

According to Christopher Lasch, it is no longer the 'revolt of the masses' that threatens 'social order and the civilising traditions of Western culture'. Instead, 'the chief threat seems to come from those at the top of the social hierarchy'. Anglo-American elites have revolted against the responsibilities of rulership. Having opened themselves up to the global economy corporate elites have become detached from traditional sources of personal, political and religious identity. Having eroded traditional folkways the world over, corporate capitalism accepts no responsibility for the spiritual decline of the West. On the contrary, educated elites treat every sign of populist resistance to globalisation as a rebirth of bigotry, intolerance and rampant racism. No one seems to believe any longer in the distinctive civilising mission of the West.

It used to be that 'the value of cultural elites lay in their willingness to assume responsibility for the exacting standards without which civilisation is impossible'. If it is to be seen as legitimate, an aristocratic elite must 'live in the service of demanding ideals'.[15] Those, such as José Ortega y Gassett, who sought to defend the aristocratic principle in the face of the democratic revolution insisted that 'Nobility is defined by the demands it makes on us - by obligations, not by rights'.[16] Today it is our cultural, political and economic elites who have made the heaviest investments in the rights industry. At the same time, those who own, manage or control the corporate economy routinely escape political responsibility for the social costs and ecological consequences of their activity. Within the global economy, the ruling class disappears behind the corporate veil while the infinitely demanding consumer is hailed as its successor. While markets register consumer preferences, polls monitor the pulse of the electorate. In fact, neither consumers, citizens nor widely dispersed individual shareholders play a significant role in a system of corporate governance dominated by markets for products, securities and corporate control. Even those in leadership positions claim no more than the ability to ride the crest of a wave of change beyond their control.

Contemporary elites are preoccupied with the relentless pursuit of their own well-being. For that they make no apologies. Those in charge of the interlocking governance structures of the corporate welfare state look forward to a future of limitless possibilities to be opened up for the rest of us by their skilful deployment of capital, labour and technology. Lasch deplores the astonishing contempt that professional, managerial and academic elites display toward the backward masses who still fear economic, cultural and technological change. All the traditions that the masses had been taught for ages to revere are suddenly up for grabs. Throughout the English-speaking world, a substantial body of educated opinion now commonly sees in the term 'Western civilisation' only 'an organised system of domination designed to enforce conformity to bourgeois values and to keep the victims of patriarchal oppression - women, children, homosexuals, people of colour - in a permanent state of subjection'.[17] Multiculturalism has become the official ideology of cosmopolitan elites more at home with their counterparts overseas than with the 'parochial prejudices' of their own heartlands. Political sophisticates in Australia, for example, reject the Eurocentric loyalties of the past, scorning the widespread attachment to the British monarchy among older Anglo-Australians. Obsessed by the need to change Australia's corporate image in support of a marketing push into Asia, politicians and business leaders, academics and artists, unite to renounce their allegiance to the British Crown. Just as Britain sacrificed Commonwealth interests on the altar of European unity, Australian opinion leaders are 'proposing that it defect from the West, redefine itself as an Asian country and cultivate close ties with its neighbours. Australia's future, they argue, is with the dynamic economies of East Asia'.[18] Elites prepared to sacrifice history, tradition and cultural identity to the cause of economic expansion are more than likely to undermine the community they profess to lead. In Canada too, the developmental dynamics of the corporate welfare state have spawned elites without any interest in the survival of their ancestral British identity. Most Canadians in leadership positions were born as British subjects. Few, if any, understand Sir John A Macdonald's determination to die a British subject. Having been placed under the disembodied dominion of the global economy by their leading politicians and businessmen, Canadians are now learning that not even their national identity can any longer be taken for granted. Within the North American free trade zone, the

Confederation regime premised on loyalty to the British Crown may face redundancy. Economic growth and development has become the overriding purpose of social life so that individuals, institutions and even nations are 'judged by the single test of how much they increase production'.[19]

A modern aristocracy of wealth incorporating a lesser nobility of brains has displaced patrician orders based upon hereditary privilege. Hereditary peerages bound by ritual solidarity with their ancestors necessarily shared a community of memory with commoners. Religion played a vital role in binding rulers and ruled through the ages. Today's elites have undermined the public power of shared remembrance by transforming the anamnestic spirit of the laws into a futuristic cult of productivity. A decent respect for the past, a sense of solidarity with our ancestors, is derided as mere nostalgia by those plugged into the currents of power. Our managerial and professional elites find their poetry in the future, not in the past.

The multi-skilled elites of the corporate welfare state retain 'many of the vices of aristocracy without its virtues'. Having drained talent away from the lower orders, the meritocratic regime breeds new forms of snobbery bereft of any sense 'of reciprocal obligations between the favoured few and the multitude'. Whatever obligations might be owed to those left behind in the scramble for social mobility have been depersonalised. Exercised through the agency of the state, the burden of discharging those responsibilities 'falls not on the professional and managerial class but, disproportionately, on the lower-middle and working class'.[20] Wage and salary earners are notoriously unable to evade the burden of taxation. At the same time, their ways of life and of earning a living remain exposed to the disruptive designs of well-meaning social engineers and coldly indifferent economic rationalists. In the name of democracy, the corporate welfare state chooses to promote a broader recruitment of elites, but not 'to raise the general level of competence, energy and devotion - "virtue" as it was called in an older political tradition'. Democracy is supposedly guaranteed by ensuring that all careers are open to the talented. In fact, as Lasch observes, 'careerism tends to undermine democracy by divorcing knowledge from practical experience, devaluing the kind of knowledge that is gained from experience and generating social conditions in which ordinary people are not expected to know anything at all'.[21] Civic virtue has been displaced by the reign of specialised expertise.

Expert knowledge is one depersonalised source of political leverage. Money is another medium for the impersonal exercise of power. Meritocracy therefore has a natural ideological affinity with the complex network of corporate plutocracies, managerial oligarchies and private autocracies dominating the institutional life of modern civil societies. Faith in the efficiency and beneficence of an economic system that allows the talented to rise to the top is an essential ingredient in the public discourse of modern social, political and corporate elites. In fact, it is the capitalist cult of the divine economy that has justified a continuing revolt of our elites against shared standards of civic obligation binding the people at large to those occupying the upper ranks. Everywhere in the Western world, political and economic elites maintain that few 'private citizens' need or desire anything more than a minimalist republic. In this brave new high-tech world, sovereignty seems to have slipped out of the hands of the people at large into an impersonal system of needs that rules over us like the omnipotent but inscrutable God of the Old Testament.

Modern capitalist society is the product of the interaction between a kind of person, a kind of economy and a kind of religion. In the early modern period, a God of Will was worshipped by the bourgeois individual of the Protestant ethic whose enterprising ways helped the modern capitalist economy take off. But, while the driven personality of the inner-directed Protestant supplied power on the runway, once in flight the economy relied on technique, not on character, to keep itself aloft. As Donald Meyer put it in his study of the American gospel of positive thinking, '[I]f at the centre of nineteenth century social imagination there had stood a man, in the twentieth he was replaced by the vision of a system.'[22]

The dominant ethos of the corporate system depends upon a novel blend of psychology, economics and theology. The economy has become an object of religious devotion for the managerial and professional classes. No wonder, Marx might have said; it is the economy alone that binds us together even as it causes 'all that is solid to melt into air'.[23] In all sectors of society and culture, economic development has become an occasion for dependency rather than belonging. Our abject subjection to the mysterious movements of the global economy parallels the relationship of Protestant believers to their 'hidden God, the God of Will' who can be known 'only in His works, not in His nature'.[24] In an awful recurrence, we are returning to the situation of the early Protestants as an abyss opens up between us and an economy invested with all the attributes of divinity. Its inner workings surpass ordinary human understanding. Among our elites and opinion leaders, insight, knowledge, and intelligence can do no more than serve the disembodied forces animating the society of perpetual growth. It is not the courage or the strength of our political and corporate leaders, nor our respect for tradition that sanctifies the system. It is faith alone. Awesome and inscrutable, spectacular and self-propelling, the system invites adoration.[25]

The End of the Democratic Revolution

In casting the corporation in 'the role of conscience-carrier of twentieth-century American society', Adolf A Berle Jr was one of many to preach the theology of corporate redemption.[26]   He saw in the American corporate system the makings of a modern City of God.   If social critics often assailed corporate America as a godless Babylon, Berle turned St. Augustine on his head by proclaiming that true justice could be realised in a corporate Zion. For St. Augustine, the kingdoms that hold us captive in Babylon are nothing 'but great robberies'.[27]   Berle denies that the corporate realm is 'soulless'. Nor is it controlled by a gang of robber barons.   In his view, there is good reason 'to anticipate that moral and intellectual leadership will appear capable of balancing our Frankenstein creations'.   The American corporate system could bring Augustine's heavenly city down to earth.   Out of the corporate decisionmaking machinery, Berle saw 'some sort of consensus of mind emerging' which is acting, 'by compulsion as it were, ... for good or ill ... surprisingly like a collective soul'.   In Berle's corporatist vision of the divine economy, the democratic nation-state was 'not to be the dominant factor' in political life.   Having brought mankind within reach of 'an evolving economic Utopia', the big business corporations are moving 'toward a greater rather than a lesser acceptance of the responsibility that goes with power'.[28]

A less sanguine observer might conclude that the age of the democratic revolution will be brought to a close by the insatiable demands of the divine economy.   In Berle's day, the American business corporation operated within a regulatory framework erected by an interventionist state responsive to the popular will.   Corporate capitalism has since expanded into a global system of needs that operates more or less freely across the boundaries that once defined and protected the democratic nation-state.   According to Benjamin Barber, the entire human race is being incorporated into 'one McWorld tied together by communications, information, entertainment and commerce'.   In mesmerising people everywhere with fast food, fast computers and fast music, McWorld has discovered that simple services to the body must be 'displaced by complex service to the soul'.   When Berle announced the apotheosis of the corporate economy, power and wealth flowed from control over the production of goods.   Today, the goods sector has been 'captured by the infotainment telesector, whose object is nothing less than the human soul'.   Postmodern capitalism sets out quite deliberately to assimilate and transform religion.   To sell American products, the corporation had to sell America: 'its popular culture, its putative prosperity, its ubiquitous imagery and software, and thus its very soul'.   Taking literally Brecht's ironic suggestion that the communist East German regime should 'dissolve the People and elect another', McWorld is recreating mankind in its own electronically graven, brand-name images.[29]

We certainly need some old-time civil religion to combat the increasingly idolatrous corporate control over the modern pathways leading from the body to the spiritual realm.[30] Unfortunately, the political theology of popular sovereignty consecrated by the early modern English, American and French revolutions is far too simplistic. It cannot cope with the extra-constitutional corporate system that has swallowed up all of the old-fashioned bourgeois liberal republics. When Rousseau and Tom Paine were articulating their respective theories of popular sovereignty, the commercial civil societies of the Western world were in their infancy. Before the American revolution, business corporations were all but unknown in the colonies and still rare enough in England to be the object of profound suspicion.[31] In those days, it was still possible to imagine civil society as an assemblage of rights-bearing individuals. Sovereignty became the legal property of a state deriving its powers from the consent of the constituent community. In principle, if not in practice, the creation of a modern democratic republic was a simple matter of common sense, requiring only that the people be recognised as the sovereign seat of all legitimate constitutional authority. The idea of popular sovereignty served as a foundational myth. Most of its framers conceived the American Constitution as a surrender of sovereign authority by the people to the governments set to rule over them in perpetuity.[32]

The possibility of making popular sovereignty anything more than a constitutional cover for the actual dominance of narrow elites has become especially remote within the highly organised, interlocking governance structures of modern corporate welfare states. In both the state and the economy, the stage of *simple* modernisation through political democratisation and the technical conquest of nature has reached its limits.[33] Just as the technologies deployed to subdue the forces of nature have become a source of growing danger to the society that created them, the eighteenth century model of popular sovereignty is too blunt an instrument to be of much use in crafting the civil constitution of a complex, transnational system of corporate capitalism. Only rarely over the past two hundred years, has a sovereign people had its democratic 'moments', suspending the rules of politics as usual to make its collective presence felt as an autonomous constitutional actor.[34] Those moments will become even fewer and farther between as the locus of political power shifts away from the liberal democratic state into a corporate overclass subordinating the peoples of the world to the increasingly risky and irresponsible dictates of the divine economy.[35]

If the political promise of modernity is to be redeemed and not squandered, the simple stage of democratisation must be succeeded by a *reflexive* constitution extending beyond the internal political order of the state into the associational life of Anglo-American civil societies. Reflexivity is the capacity to refine and reflect upon one's own preferences. Reflexive preferences would be the outcome of the conscious confrontation of one's own point of view with an opposing point of view, or of the multiplicity of viewpoints that the citizen [or the bourgeois], upon reflection, is likely to discover within his or her own self'.[36] An enhanced capacity for reflexivity could be built into the corporate sector by requiring the investor as *bourgeois* to confront the investor as *citizen* in the governance of corporations responsible for important matters of public policy. A reflexive constitution must create a civic role for the corporate bourgeoisie. Otherwise the ossified traditions of Anglo-American republicanism will crumble into dust. Contemporary nation-states are running a chronic democratic deficit; their electoral rituals have become mere sideshows in a world governed by the imperial expansion of the corporate system. In place of real constitutional reform, we have the pious rhetoric of a minimalist republicanism indifferent to the proliferation of powerful elites prone to regular displays of bad institutional citizenship.

If the historic gains of the democratic revolution are to be preserved, the best citizens among substantial shareholders must be allowed and encouraged to constitute themselves as a civic elite within the corporate institutions of modern capitalist societies. Otherwise, widespread cynicism over the irresponsible exercise of corporate power and the corrupt influence of corporate money are bound to erode popular confidence in parliament, the press and public life generally. Given the collective action problems that have always plagued the many, only the public-spirited few are likely to mount an effective challenge to the culture of narcissism now dominant within the ruling elites.[37] By reinventing the aristocratic principle and applying it to the governance of the corporation, a republican constitutional order could help us cope with the multiplying risks generated by a global society of perpetual growth. When the major task of capitalist development was the conquest of scarcity it made good sense to privilege the private benefits of corporate share ownership over the public burdens and civic challenges associated with membership in a corporate body politic. That policy gave top billing to the maximisation of private wealth. Not surprisingly then, the public sphere formally constituted within the corporate body politic became an empty shell. General meetings of shareholders offered few opportunities for deliberative or democratic decision-making. Having ceased to be little republics, corporations came to be ruled in a plutocratic, oligarchical or simply autocratic manner. Within the constitution of the corporation, the bourgeois enjoyed economic, political and even spiritual hegemony. Meanwhile the citizen was confined to the few public spaces organised around and within the state.

It is high time to tilt the constitutional balance within the corporation away from civic privatism by creating a political role for the active investor. A new emphasis on the political character of membership in the corporate body politic would attach civic responsibilities to the proprietary rights of share ownership. It may be that relatively few individuals among millions of widely dispersed investors in thousands of firms are likely to take up those responsibilities. Not everyone is moved by the joys of public happiness. But all those who do value the political privileges of membership should stand on an equal footing in the body politic bearing final responsibility for the good governance of the corporate enterprise. Active investors should engage in a process of deliberative decision-making on matters within the reach of their authority[38] on the basis of one voice, one vote. The plutocratic principle of one share, one vote would cease to hollow out the civic significance of corporate governance.

Only under conditions of political equality can any significant number of shareholders hope to overcome the formidable collective action problems facing activists within any corporate governance regime. Where one's voice is proportional to one's economic stake in the corporate enterprise, shareholder activists become an endangered species. Even if all of the members of a dispersed group of shareholders share a common interest in obtaining some collective benefit, 'they have no common interest in paying the cost of providing that collective good'. As Mancur Olson points out, the rational self-interest of each member will lead him to 'prefer that the others pay the entire cost', especially when he 'would get any benefit provided whether he had borne part of the cost or not'.[39] Under the one-share, one-vote regime of corporate governance, even the most public-spirited shareholders have little incentive to work for collective goods that flow to the whole body of shareholders. If their stake in the enterprise is relatively modest, they will be able to capture only a disproportionately small share of the collective benefit, while bearing a disproportionately large share of the burden of providing that public good.

Olson's argument is based upon a bleak view of human motivation. Shareholder behaviour responds only to the bourgeois calculus of individual self-interest.   Action aimed at the attainment of a collective good will be more or less likely depending upon the burdens or costs that must be borne by the actor.   Unless his share of the public benefits gained outweighs the private costs incurred, or the activity permits the acquisition of additional individual, noncollective goods such as social status or social acceptance, the rational individual will not bestir himself.   From this perspective the role of the citizen is defined by the burdens and sacrifices it imposes upon the individual.   Once the preferences of citizens become as fixed and predictable as those of the bourgeois, the democratic revolution will have succumbed to the unchallenged lordship of capital.

Civilising Capitalism

But civic action has at least two dimensions: the expressive and the communicative.[40]   Reasoned deliberation within a community of political peers does call for disinterested discussion and debate aimed at persuasion and accommodation.   Even if we were all born altruists, political communication would generate private costs as well as public benefits.   But collective action also creates a dramatic setting where individuals can give expression to the heroic or agonistic side of their being.[41]   By appearing together in public, individuals compete for glory and recognition in the eyes of their peers.   That agonistic striving allows citizens to disclose who they are.   Acting to overcome the futility and mortality of one's life through the performance of exemplary deeds is not simply a form of self-denial or self-sacrifice.   On the contrary, the agonistic dimension of citizenship offers the real possibility of self-fulfilment, along with the dramatic risk of personal disaster.   Nor is it at all obvious that the joys of public happiness are experienced as a private, noncollective good.   In politics, as in theatre, the play's the thing.   Many of the benefits reaped by both actors and audiences from an accomplished dramatic or political performance are intrinsic to the interaction between actors and audience.

   If Aristotle was right in claiming that man is a political animal,[42] civic action may not be motivated solely by the hope of extrinsic rewards but also by the opportunity to exercise in public powers of reasoned speech and dramatic action.   For every speaker there must be a listener.   For every actor there must be an audience.   The converse is also true.   Listening or gathering together to form an audience is pointless if no one is prepared to step forward to speak or act in public.   The very willingness to engage in civic action, even if only by becoming part of the audience, helps to constitute a public sphere within which all of us can realise an untapped human potential.

The problem with the governance of corporations as they are presently constituted is that only money talks. Those who hold a majority of the voting shares in a corporate general meeting, even if they are only a small minority of the persons present, have no need either to speak or to listen to their fellow members. Effective civic action is made even more difficult by the use of proxies, allowing members who choose not to participate in debates over matters of common concern to delegate their voting power to others (usually a representative of an incumbent control or management grouping). Even the best corporate citizen is bound to be discouraged by a voting regime that systematically devalues the power of reasoned speech in favour of the sheer dumb weight of proprietary interest. This would not amount to a constitutional issue if the process of corporate decision-making affected only private economic interests. But corporations now exercise powers that are governmental or political in character. A more reflexive form of decision-making is now necessary. Corporate governance could be reconstituted to allow shareholders to become responsible, energetic and devoted members of a joint enterprise. In effect, we could end the presumption that shareholders dissatisfied with the performance of the corporation will follow the Wall Street rule and sell out. Exit makes sense when the individual shareholder has no effective voice in corporate governance. But, if all shareholders possessing a minimum property qualification or threshold stake in an enterprise were guaranteed an effective political voice in its governance, loyalty could replace exit as the most rational response to a downturn in corporate fortunes.[43] This would provide a republican version of the 'patient capital' characteristic of Japanese corporatism, where liquidity is unavailable to investors who participate in control.[44] In the republican model, control would be vested in a body of natural persons, not in the faceless coalition of institutional investors making up the Japanese *keiretsu*. Money managers are not principals. Their direct role in corporate governance should be determined by the force of their arguments and the weight of their experience, not by the size of their portfolios. Under a reformed regime, institutional investors would still retain the right to take a Wall Street walk. Nor would the new arrangements prevent concerned money managers from becoming individual investors in their own right. Under these circumstances, the most committed individual shareholders would become, in effect, a sort of natural aristocracy within the corporate body politic. In this way, it would be possible to introduce the aristocratic principle into the total constitutional order of the corporate welfare state.   But, in another paradox, the reinvention of aristocracy becomes possible only when constitutional recognition is given to the democratic principle of political equality in the governance of the modern business corporation.

The point of such a move would not be to reverse the historical process by which ruling elites have been transformed from 'a committee of landlords'[45] into a capitalist class and later still into the mere embodiment of a vast impersonal system of needs.   Rather, the object would be to attach effective and legitimate constitutional authority to the ownership of corporate property. Landed property was once understood as the indispensable material foundation for the freedom and independence of the citizen.   It was not however the medium through which the civic virtues were cultivated or practised.[46]   The rise of the corporate system has utterly transformed the nature of property. Ownership once signified a form of personal dominion over the external things of the world.   Corporate shares do not denote a relation between persons and things.   Rather they establish a complex set of relationships between persons[47] in whose name managerial agents exercise an impersonal dominion over other persons and things inside as well as outside the firm.   In principle, it is now possible to create a genuinely reflexive constitutional order by carving out new civic spaces within the corporate domain.

Corporate property provides the essential institutional medium for new forms of citizenship which build into joint enterprises the capacity to reflect on the nature and consequences of their own activity.   Matters such as selecting the CEO, electing boards of directors, approving executive compensation and the definition of basic corporate goals could be decided on the basis of one person, one vote by all shareholders meeting a minimum property qualification.   In the political process surrounding such corporate decisions, money would still be talking but only through the medium of natural persons each with a single vote. Under these conditions, some individuals might be tempted to sacrifice their limited financial stake in a particular enterprise to serve other political or private interests.   But most active investors will want to increase the value of their own investment in the firm. If so, they will pay attention when money does talk. If they refuse to obey the laws of the market place, fools and idealists will not only pay a financial penalty themselves, they will destroy the savings of other economic innocents who choose to ignore the advice, the warnings or the threats of large investors aiming only to maximise their wealth. On the other hand, the experience of having to persuade their peers may lead shareholders of all descriptions to discover hitherto unknown civic skills and interests.

Over time, one can imagine a new class of corporate notables coming into being. Propertied persons could trade less diversity in their investment portfolios for the opportunity to play an active civic role in the governance of a narrower range of corporate enterprises. By treating shareholders as political equals in fundamental corporate decisions, constitutional law would help the bourgeois and the citizen to learn the art of corporate governance from each other. If the corporation is to survive and prosper while doing business in a responsible and enlightened manner, a coalition of interests must learn to balance the economic imperatives which call the business corporation into being with the responsible exercise of its governmental powers. The sort of people who develop and share that level of practical and political understanding would deserve to be recognised as a sort of republican aristocracy.

Corporate Governance and Republican Political Theory

It is worth noting that while Hannah Arendt might have considered the idea of republican society oxymoronic, she saw nothing amiss in the notion of a republican aristocracy. Unfortunately, she never developed a clear idea of how such a civic elite could be constituted within a highly organised, modern civil society. By enhancing the prestige attached to membership in the corporate body politic, we could reinvigorate the ancient aristocratic ideal of civic virtue while simultaneously opening up new constitutional spaces for the democratic principle of equality. The constitution of the corporation can be conceived as a sort of mixed polity balancing private ownership interests against the public responsibilities of membership in a corporate body possessed of both economic wealth and political power. A modernised, civic aristocracy could emerge if corporate governance is reconstituted to include a political theatre in which bourgeois investors keeping a sharp eye on their own interests can also take on the role of citizens striving to distinguish themselves in the service of the common good (and vice versa). Within the corporate body politic there will be room, as well, for the vital role of kingship. Someone must provide the leadership essential to any great enterprise, from the Trojan War to the marketing of computer software. Entrepreneurial talent is an authentic expression of kingship within the corporate life of a pluralistic modern society.[48]

Arendt was perhaps too pessimistic in concluding that the modern realm of the social must be driven solely by the economic logic of necessity.[49] In fact the corporate economy generates substantial political power. That political power can and should be constitutionalised. The first step in that direction is to speak of corporate governance in the civic language of political theory. Academic and professional discussions of corporate governance have for too long been conducted in the quintessentially bourgeois language of economics. Corporations are not simply private economic or accounting units of capital accumulation. Nor are they mere legal fictions. They are undeniably real and very powerful social institutions as well. Even in the academic literature on corporate governance, recognition is growing of the organisational and institutional power wielded by the corporate sector.[50] It no longer seems so obvious that the development of corporate law simply reflects the more or less autonomous economic logic of efficiency. But the reality of corporate power is not just an objective empirical fact; it also has the capacity to shape, or to undermine, our normative universe, the *nomos* that lies at the heart of every great legal civilisation.[51] For that reason, the law still requires shareholders to play a special constitutional role denied to other stakeholders. On a cynical reading of corporate law, shareholders are included in the official, corporate decision-making process less because they are indispensable providers of capital than because they lend a veneer of constitutional legitimacy to managerial power.[52] A more reflective approach would emphasise the moral resources that shareholders possess even in their present degraded condition. The manifest existence of unfettered managerial power cries out for normative justification and constitutional balancing. But shareholders are now ill-equipped to serve as constitutional counterweights to professional managers. We need new forms of corporate governance designed to produce, not just power and profits, but legitimate constitutional authority as well.

The corporate constitution cannot be reduced, in other words, to a contractual mechanism intended purely and simply to maximise long-term corporate value.[53] Nor should the constitution of the corporation as a powerful social organisation become an autolegitimating end in itself.[54] Corporations produce more than economic value for shareholders and power for managers; they also generate risks for the world at large for which some body or persons should have to accept effective political responsibility. Whatever form the corporate constitution takes, it remains the product of political and constitutional as well as economic choices. According to the ancient doctrine of politics, the most elementary choices facing the constituent power were between monarchy, aristocracy and democracy. The ideal polity would strike a stable balance between the one, the few and the many. A latter-day Aristotle would not find many contemporary corporate constitutions that could be classified as aristocracies and fewer still that could qualify as shareholder democracies. But examples of executive tyranny, plutocratic corruption and managerial oligarchy are plentiful enough in the corporate jungle. If the corporate constitution offered a place for the citizen as well as the bourgeois, managerial oligarchies and other accustomed modes of plutocratic dominion could give way to a genuinely noble aristocracy of talent. Similarly, authentic entrepreneurial forms of kingship would degenerate less often into petty corporate tyrannies. Corporate governance need not remain forever a domain ruled in the name of passive investors by managerial surrogates who listen only when money talks. It may still be possible to govern corporations in the public interest without relying solely upon the heavy hand of the nanny state. That alternative, republican strategy of constitutional reform would aim to create vital public realms within most important corporate enterprises. By embedding the property interests of owners in a civic process of corporate decision-making open to all active members, a balance could be achieved between the self-interested pursuit of long-term corporate value and the responsible management of socially shared risks. Once we recognise that the corporation can and should be constitutionalised, we can see that the idea of a modern republican society is not, after all, a contradiction in terms.

Indeed, Arendt's own frankly aristocratic model of council democracy helps to clarify how and why one might expect to find a new role for the *citizen* alongside and within the *bourgeois* in the modern business corporation. So far as I know, Arendt never gave much, if any, sustained thought to corporate governance. Had she done so, she might have seen the need for new forms of the civil bodies politic she so admired in the colonial history of the American republic. The Mayflower Compact was an embryonic form of the little republics that could be constituted within modern corporate enterprises. If all those with a significant property stake in a joint enterprise could gain entrance, on the basis of equality, to the corporate public sphere, a new civic aristocracy could be selected or, as Arendt put it, 'would select itself'.[55]

Like those who participated in the council democracy that emerged spontaneously during the Hungarian revolution of 1956, this self-selecting aristocracy would be an elite 'of the people and sprung from the people', but they would not be 'nominated from above or supported from below'. Those who selected themselves would be 'those who cared and those who took the initiative'. Whatever authority they acquired would rest 'on nothing but the confidence of their equals'. This equality would not be natural, but rather political. It would not be something that members of this new civic elite would have been born with, it would be 'the equality of those who [have] committed themselves to, and now [are] engaged in a joint enterprise'. Only those who 'have demonstrated that they care for more than their private happiness and are concerned about the state of the world would have the right to be heard in the conduct' of corporate business. If those who belong to this self-selected aristocracy of corporate citizens 'are self-chosen, then those who do not belong are self-excluded'. Arendt points out that such self-exclusion 'far from being arbitrary discrimination, would in fact give substance and reality to one of the most important negative liberties we have enjoyed since the end of the ancient world, namely, freedom from politics'.[56]

Our problem is that corporate elites have freed themselves only from *constitutional* politics. Corporate politics continues as a secretive affair conducted in corridors and behind closed doors. In practical political terms, no universal and comprehensive solution to the problem of corporate responsibility is likely to emerge so long as most private corporations deliver on the promise of prosperity. Things may turn out differently in major enterprises affected with a substantial public interest. In many industries, participation in corporate governance is a burden shareholders would rather not shoulder. In others, active investors will feel duty bound to discharge their civic obligations faithfully and well. The highly visible media business, for example, offers public-spirited investors the chance to express the heroic or agonistic side of their nature while others will be enticed by the prospect of financial reward. Both might be surprised to discover how malleable their preferences turn out to be. Republican political theory helps us to understand the opportunities (and risks) of civic action. But we also need to establish that there is a genuine constitutional or political need for a self-selecting aristocracy in the realm of corporate governance. Even more urgently we need to identify the economic limits to politics in the modern corporate welfare state.

Notes

1   Tom Nairn discusses the strange 'Ukanian' blend of patrician glamour and popular backwardness lending a fairy-tale aura of romantic archaism to the British constitution in *The Enchanted Glass: Britain and Its Monarchy* (London: Radius, 1989).

2   Joseph de Maistre, *Considerations on France*, tr. Richard A Lebrun (Montreal: McGill-Queen's University Press, 1974) pp 44-5.

3   Claus Offe and Ulrich K Preuss, 'Democratic Institutions and Moral Resources' in David Held, ed, *Political Theory Today* (Oxford: Polity Press, 1991) p 167.

4   Hannah Arendt, *The Human Condition* (Chicago: University of Chicago Press, 1958), pp 38-49; Offe and Preuss, *supra* note 3 at p 169.

5   Hannah Arendt, *On Revolution* (Harmondsworth: Pelican, 1973) p 253.

6   George Winterton, *Monarchy to Republic: Australian Republican Government* (Melbourne: Oxford University Press, 1986).

7   Republic Advisory Committee, *An Australian Republic: The Options - The Report* (The Report of the Republic Advisory Committee, 1993).

8   *Ibid*; *Australian Capital Television v The Commonwealth* (*Political Advertising* case) (1992) 66 *Australian Law Journal Reports* 695.

9   Polybius, *The Rise of the Roman Empire* (Harmondsworth: Penguin, 1979); P P Craig, *Public Law and Democracy in the United Kingdom and the United States* (Oxford: Clarendon Press, 1990).

10   Ged Martin, *Bunyip Aristocracy* (Sydney: Croom Helm, 1986).

11   Albert Venn Dicey, *Introduction to the Study of the Law of the Constitution* (London: Macmillan, 1948).

12   Louis Hartz, *The Liberal Tradition in America: An Interpretation of American Political Thought Since the American Revolution* (New York: Harcourt, 1955).

13   Gordon S Wood, *The Radicalism of the American Revolution* (New York: Vintage, 1991) p 276.

14   *Ibid* pp 243, 341.

15   Christopher Lasch, *The Revolt of the Elites and the Betrayal of Democracy* (New York: Norton, 1995) pp 25-6.

16   José Ortega y Gasset, *The Revolt of the Masses* (London: Unwin, 1961) p 48.

17   Lasch, *supra* note 15 at p 26.

18   Samuel P Huntington, 'The Clash of Civilizations' *Foreign Affairs* (Summer 1993) p 45.

19   Lasch, *supra* note 15 at p 42.

20   *Ibid,* pp 44-5.

21   *Ibid,* p 79.

22   Donald Meyer, *The Positive Thinkers: A Study of the American Quest for Health, Wealth and Personal Power from Mary Baker Eddy to Norman Vincent Peale* (Garden City, NY: Anchor, 1966) p 177.

23   Karl Marx and Friedrich Engels, 'The Manifesto of the Communist Party' in *The Essential Left: Four Classic Texts on the Principles of Socialism* (London: Unwin, 1960) p 18.

24   Meyer, *supra* note 22 at p 177.

25   *Ibid,* p 178; see also Guy Debord, *The Society of the Spectacle* (Detroit: Black and Red, 1970).

26   Adolf A Berle, Jr, *The 20th Century Capitalist Revolution* (New York: Harcourt, Brace & Co, 1954) p 182.

27   Henry Paolucci, ed, *The Political Writings of St. Augustine* (Chicago: Gateway, 1962) pp 28-29.

28   Berle, *supra* note 26 at pp 183, 187, 175, 174, 173. Cf Scott R Bowman, *The Modern Corporation and American Political Thought: Law, Power and Ideology* (University Park: Pennsylvania State University Press, 1996) pp 203-217.

29   Benjamin R Barber, *Jihad vs McWorld: How Globalism and Tribalism are Reshaping the World* (New York: Ballantine, 1996) pp 4, 60, 78; Bertolt Brecht, 'The Solution', in Martin Esslin, *Brecht: A Choice of Evils* (London: Mercury, 1965) p 165.

30   Barber, *supra* note 29 at p 60.

31   Joseph S Davis, *Essays in the Earlier History of American Corporations* Vol II (Cambridge, MA: Harvard University Press, 1917) pp 3-6; Armand du Bois, *The English Business Company After the Bubble Act* (New York: Octagon, 1971).

32   Gordon S Wood, *The Creation of the American Republic, 1776-1787* (New York: Norton, 1972); *Luther v Borden* (1849) 48 US (7 How) 1 (US Supreme Court); George M Dennison, *The Dorr War: Republicanism on Trial, 1831-1861* (Lexington: University Press of Kentucky, 1976); Elizabeth Mensch and Alan Freeman, 'A Republican Agenda for Hobbesian America?' (1989) 41 *Florida Law Review* 581.

33   Ulrich Beck, *Risk Society: Towards a New Modernity*, tr. Mark Ritter (London: Sage, 1992).

34   James Grey Pope, 'Republican Moments: The Role of Direct Popular Power in the American Constitutional Order' (1990) 139 *University of Pennsylvania Law Review* 287.

35   Beck, *supra* note 33.

36   Offe and Preuss, *supra* note 3 at p 170.

37   Christopher Lasch, *The Culture of Narcissism: American Life in an Age of Diminishing Expectations* (New York: Norton, 1978).

38   Under the current regime, most academic commentators believe that managers and boards of directors are more likely 'to act for common shareholder wealth than shareholders' themselves.   The authority of shareholders within the corporate constitution is therefore sharply limited.   See, Jeffrey N Gordon, 'Shareholder Initiative: A Social Choice and Game Theoretic Approach to Corporate Law' (1991) 60 *University of Cincinnati Law Review* 347.   If the game of corporate politics were played according to republican rules, the reach of shareholder authority would expand as active investors learned how to recognise and realise their common interest in good corporate governance.   The optimal balance between shareholder authority and managerial power in corporate bodies politic reconstituted as little republics will be discovered through trial and error not prior prescription.

39   Mancur Olson, *The Logic of Collective Action* (Cambridge MA: Harvard University Press, 1971) p 21.

40   Maurizio Passerin d'Entrèves, *The Political Philosophy of Hannah Arendt* (London: Routledge, 1994) p 153.

41   Arendt, *supra* note 4 at pp 175-87.

42   Aristotle, *The Politics,* tr. T A Sinclair (Harmondsworth: Penguin, 1951) p 59.

43   Albert O Hirschman, *Exit, Voice and Loyalty: Responses to Decline in Firms, Organizations and State* (Cambridge MA: Harvard University Press, 1970).

44   John C Coffee Jr, 'Liquidity versus Control: The Institutional Investor as Corporate Monitor' (1991) 91 *Columbia Law Review* 1277 at p 1296.

45   Barrington Moore Jr, *Social Origins of Dictatorship and Democracy* (Boston: Beacon Press, 1967) pp 18-20.

46   J G A Pocock, 'Cambridge Paradigms and Scotch Philosophers: A Study of the Relations between the Civic Humanist and the Civil Jurisprudential Interpretation of Eighteenth-Century Social Thought' in Istvan Hont and Michael Ignatieff, eds, *Wealth and Virtue: The Shaping of Political Economy in the Scottish Enlightenment* (Cambridge: Cambridge University Press, 1983) p 248.

47   Kenneth Vandevelde, 'The New Property of the Nineteenth Century: The Development of the Modern Concept of Property' (1980) 29 *Buffalo Law Review* 325.

48   Cf Margaret Canovan, *Hannah Arendt: A Reinterpretation of Her Political Thought* (Cambridge: Cambridge University Press, 1994) p 207.

49   Arendt, *supra* note 4.

50   Lynne L Dallas, 'Two Models of Corporate Governance: Beyond Berle and Means' (1988) 22 *University of Michigan Journal of Law Reform* 19; William W Bratton, 'The Economic Structure of the Post-Contractual Corporation' (1992) 87 *Northwestern University Law Review* 180 at p 197.

51   Robert Cover, 'Foreword: 1982 Term, *Nomos* and Narrative' (1983) 97 *Harvard Law Review* 4.

52   Dallas, *supra* note 50 at p 94.

53   Frank J Easterbrook and Daniel R Fischel, *The Economic Structure of Corporate Law* (Cambridge MA: Harvard University Press, 1991) pp 1-39.

54   Cf Dallas, *supra* note 50.

55   Arendt, *supra* note 5 at p 277.

56   *Ibid,* pp 277-80.

2 Corporations and the Economic Logic of Efficiency

Introduction

Monarchy and aristocracy occasionally persist as residual traces of ancient constitutions incorporating the presumptively natural social orders of a mixed and balanced polity. Nevertheless, every Western nation-state now grounds its political legitimacy in the democratic principle of popular sovereignty. Even in the United Kingdom, the royal family and the hereditary peerage face the threat of extinction. The demos reigns supreme. But this does not mean that the people actually rule. On the contrary, the modern corporate welfare state spawns a complex interlocking network of professional, managerial, financial and political elites. It has long since been evident that 'the organisational reality of any modern state is radically incompatible with its being a system of popular rule'.[1] As Joseph de Maistre put it, 'the people which *command* are not the people which *obey*'.[2]

But what leads a notionally sovereign people to lapse into the habits of obedience characteristic of a bourgeois liberal republic? Why is the modern demos unable to 'enjoy the liberty of the ancients, which consisted in an active and constant participation in collective power'? Benjamin Constant answered that the experience of civic freedom is not all it is cracked up to be by strong republicans. Men paid a heavy price for their participation in a collective body of citizens. '[A]lmost always sovereign in public affairs', the citizen 'was a slave in all his private relations'. Citizens of the modern bourgeois liberal republic are 'far more attached than the ancients to [their] individual independence'.[3] As a consequence, modern states enjoy popular legitimacy not because they contrive to provide the people with 'greater scope for sovereign agency, but rather because they furnish the great majority of citizens with the security and prosperity to live their lives as they please'.[4] Individual preferences loom large in the modern calculus of political consent. But, as John Dunn observes, 'every modern demos also requires a dependable tide of goods and services on which to deploy its preferences'. The systemic need to ensure 'that this tide will indeed continue to run' imposes the pervasive economic limits to political action within the bourgeois liberal republic.[5]

For citizens and rulers alike 'the choice of effective economic policies is, under normal conditions, the most important and permanent of modern political needs'.[6] Since the eighteenth century, the use of the corporation in business has presented 'important questions of public policy to be resolved through legal processes'. The main thrust of public policies has been to treat the corporation to a sort of legal technology providing 'firm central direction for the enterprising use of pooled assets'. The legitimacy of the modern business corporation is tied to its role 'as a socially useful instrument of economic growth'.[7] Within this policy framework, the constitutional arrangements for the internal governance of the corporation are justified purely on the basis of their economic utility. In law, the business corporation is no longer routinely recognised as a body politic exercising governmental powers; instead it is conceived as a private economic unit of capital accumulation. In theory, legal regulation aims to promote patterns of managerial and shareholder behaviour that will enhance the firm's economic value.

Nowhere is that economistic and utilitarian understanding of the modern business corporation more deeply entrenched than in the United States. It is bound to seem somewhat surprising then that the law of the early American republic recognised the corporate charter as the constitution of a civil body politic. Even though they soon came to be labelled 'private' institutions,[8] business corporations possessed a number of constitutional features that could not be understood solely in terms of their economic utility. First, they were created by a special act of incorporation. The economic and financial interests at stake in a business corporation may have been private. Nevertheless that corporation was a creature of the state legislature enacting its charter. Not surprisingly, these early business corporations were often vested with public service functions. Turnpikes and roads existed not just to increase the private wealth of their owners but also to provide valuable and important services to the community. Even banks and insurance companies were understood as hybrid amalgams of private interests and public purposes. Its charter endowed each corporation with a specific raison d'être. By requiring unanimous shareholder approval for any change to the essential character of a joint enterprise, the doctrine of *ultra vires* preserved the distinctive political identity of the corporation.[9] Left to itself, the legal logic of economic utility reduces the corporation to a mere thing of wax, enabling managers to exploit whatever business opportunities come their way. But, so long as the corporate charter was once likened to the constitution of a little republic, the membership conferred by share ownership carried with it political responsibility for the conduct of corporate business. As late as 1837, one could find judicial support for the proposition that all members of the corporation were entitled at common law to vote on the basis of one person, one vote. Much more frequently, there was legislative support for caps on the voting power of large shareholders. It was not simply taken for granted that the weight of one's voice and vote in the conduct of corporate affairs should depend upon the relative size of one's equity stake in the enterprise.[10]

The Erosion Thesis

By 1840, however, the corporation had already lost much of its republican character. Jacksonian democracy gave free rein to the expansionist forces of liberal capitalism. A potent combination of moneyed interests, radical populism and its own internal contradictions deformed the embryonic republican model of the corporation as a civil body politic. Before long special charters had been replaced by general incorporation laws. With the collapse of the *ultra vires* doctrine and the unchallenged hegemony of the one share, one vote rule, the corporation lost its constitutional identity as a body politic. The formal structures of corporate governance became an empty shell. The elaborate legal rituals surrounding general meetings, shareholder voting rights, the election of boards of directors and so on served mainly to relieve 'private' investors of both political responsibility and financial liability for their firm's corporate activities by centralising control over their pooled assets. In the governance of the corporation, the presumptively shared, plutocratic interests of all shareholders are now served by a managerial elite with its own stake in the profitability of the enterprises they control. With the growth of national and then international capital markets the transformation of the entrepreneurial owner into a passive investor was completed.

In the legal historiography of the American business corporation, the story just recounted is what Walter Werner called the 'erosion thesis'.[11] Adolf Berle and Louis Brandeis were the most influential proponents of that interpretation of corporate legal history. While they gave sharply contrasting accounts of the erosion process, both men 'concurred on a fundamental proposition: ownership of the corporation had become divorced from control as the states' original strict regulation had shrivelled and disappeared'.[12]

Brandeis's version of the story emphasised the relationship between the states and corporations and not the linkage between shareholders and management within the corporation. For Brandeis, the state had abdicated its sovereign responsibility for the governance and regulation of its corporate creations.[13] Berle, on the other hand, 'looked inside the corporation to show how shareholders had lost their original rights and control position'.[14] In Berle's narrative, an original shareholder democracy of active owners in small firms embodied the traditional logic of property and profits. The irresistible forces propelling the growth of the modern public corporation hollowed out a corporate constitution that presupposed the unity of ownership and control. Characterised by a wide diffusion of share ownership, the modern corporation depends upon a new class of professional managers holding relatively small personal equity stakes in their 'own' enterprise.[15]

If the corporation had once been an association of owners controlling their pooled assets on terms closely scrutinised and supervised by the state, it is now a private contractual arrangement through which many individuals contribute to a pool of capital under centralised management and control. Under these circumstances, widely dispersed shareholders face formidable collective action problems should they ever feel the need to challenge those who exercise effective control over corporate assets and activities. Individual shareholders will not be inclined to devote significant resources to the task of monitoring managerial performance if they will only receive a small proportion of whatever collective goods their enhanced individual efforts might produce. Every rational maximiser of utilities would prefer to be a free rider on the civic-minded efforts of others, even if significant collective goods might be foregone through a failure to act.[16]

Effective monitoring, so the managerial thesis goes, is expensive. Why should any particular investor incur that cost if he can benefit costlessly from someone else's public-spirited efforts? The disincentives to shareholder action in the early American republic would have been formidable even under the most republican regime of shareholders rights. Shareholders scattered across several towns, counties or even states would have found it extraordinarily difficult and impossibly inconvenient to communicate with each other outside the forum of a general meeting. Once the factional interests of large shareholders were secured by the one share, one vote rule, it became economically irrational for small investors to play an active role in corporate governance. At shareholder's meetings only a small minority of members would be present. Through control of the proxy machinery and the nomination of directors, managerial elites came to secure their dominance within modern business corporations.

The practical irrelevance of the shareholders meeting to the everyday governance of the modern corporation reflects the separation of ownership from control that became its hallmark.   Ownership once united the entrepreneurial attributes of financial risk-taking with managerial responsibility.   Only when the interests of ownership and the powers of control are more or less fused in a single decision-maker can the corporation effectively perform the economic role of the entrepreneur.   From a strictly economic point of view, the separation of ownership and control is problematic because it bifurcates 'the identity of the entrepreneur into owners and managers'.[17] If those who manage corporate assets cannot be effectively monitored by those who own the enterprise, long-term profitability may suffer.

It should be obvious that Berle was no corporate republican.   The problem of corporate governance posed by the separation of ownership and control was portrayed as economic, not constitutional.   Berle employed a simple entrepreneurial model of the firm in which the corporation enjoys an unquestioned legitimacy so long as it serves as an efficient means of mobilising large amounts of capital from many sources.   But, if managers come to enjoy a discretionary power to pursue goals other than long-term profitability, Berle acknowledged that the legitimacy of the modern corporation would come into question.   If it proved impossible to restore a measure of shareholder control, not only might the entrepreneurial effectiveness of the firm suffer as managers indulged their own interests, but there might be a real need for governmental intervention to ensure the socially responsible exercise of corporate power.   But however active a shareholder might become in corporate governance, Berle assumes that he will be moved by the entrepreneurial logic of profit and not by any civic need to participate in authority.[18]

The Inherence Thesis

The legal literature on corporate governance is dominated by the bedrock assumption, shared by almost everyone who seems to matter, that business corporations are 'economic institutions that by and large have served us well'. Few dispute the standard view of the big corporation as 'the most effective device, not only for aggregating capital, but also for freeing managers to use that capital effectively'.[19] There is, however, an ongoing dispute between the erosion theorists and other scholars who deny that shareholders were ever actively interested in the governance of the American business corporation. Some scholars claim that the relationship between owners and managers has not undergone fundamental change. Walter Werner, for example, offers 'a view of the corporate past that stresses the inherent nature of the public corporation's governance structure and a continuous maturation of such corporations, not a conversion from close to public corporations'. In Werner's account, the separation of ownership from control can be seen in the very first corporations where shareholders were just as supine as they are today. He concludes that what he calls the inherence thesis, 'unlike the erosion doctrine, mirrors the facts of history'.[20]

Werner's inherence thesis carries significant implications for current debates over corporate governance. If shareholders have always been passive investors, they must be inherently incapable of and uninterested in exercising effective control over managers. Since there was never a period in the legal history of the corporation when shareholders were interested in playing an active role in monitoring managerial performance, it makes little sense to develop reform proposals designed to expand the rights of shareholders to participate in corporate governance. Instead, corporate law should aim only to facilitate effective performance of the utility functions for which the corporation is best suited. Corporations, on this view, 'have developed a unique capability for producing goods and services efficiently'. That capability can best be utilised 'in an environment of competition in markets for products, capital and corporate control'. So long as the law preserves 'a free, fair and informed market that allows him to exit from the corporation when he believes it is to his interest to make an exit', the shareholder will remain inherently and obstinately bourgeois.[21] There is therefore no point to treating the passive investor in a private business corporation as a public-spirited citizen.

As one might expect, the most prominent proponents of the inherence doctrine have been scholars associated with the law and economics movement. For these writers, the legal history of the corporation before the first wide public promotions of American railroads holds little interest. The older law often portrayed civil corporations, whatever their purpose or character, as little republics. But the legal forms and civic language appropriate to the governance of a civil body politic had little functional significance for the large business corporations emerging under the auspices of Jacksonian democracy. Henry G Manne claims that the modern American business corporation 'came into existence because entrepreneurs, or promoters, needed some device to raise capital from a relatively large number of investors'. To an economist, the growth of centralised forms of corporate management and control is the inescapable corollary of 'the central concept of the corporation as a capital-raising device'.[22] Understanding investors and investment becomes the sole province of economic theory.

Democratic Capitalism and the Legalised Flight from Responsibility

But it is not only neo-conservative champions of 'democratic capitalism' who deny the relevance of political theory or constitutional jurisprudence to corporate governance. Even loyal workhorses of the social democratic left such as Harry Glasbeek refuse to recognise the existence of a real problem. In his view, cases of 'wrongful corporate behaviour' are usually 'a clear violation of existing legal standards' or the result of the externalisation of enterprise costs. In either case, 'this could be taken care of by the existing legal systems without requiring any changes in corporate governance'. For Glasbeek, it makes good economic and legal sense finally to acknowledge that the corporation is nothing more than 'a device to further capital accumulation and selfish profit-maximisation'.[23] But while the law and economics movement treats profit maximisation as a positive good, Glasbeek regards profit-making activities as a necessary evil. Werner, Manne and Daniel Fischel all look to markets for products, capital, managerial services and corporate control to ensure that corporations continue to perform their essential function: the creation of wealth and the unlocking of value.[24] Glasbeek looks instead to the power of the state. Both camps employ the rhetoric of democracy to justify the revolt of professional, managerial and ideological elites against legally binding standards of corporate social and political responsibility.

For Glasbeek, reforms should aim not to restructure the internal governance of the corporation but 'to recapture democratic control over the state'. Because corporations have become 'central to the economy and thus to the polity', the electorate has been effectively disempowered. Glasbeek claims that 'the problem is one of too little democracy', but this turns out to mean that the sovereignty of the *state* 'is diminished because governments must, in the first place, respond to the needs of dominant economic actors'.[25] Re-empowering the democratic electorate becomes possible only by injecting new vigour into the therapeutic and interventionist arms of the corporate welfare state. But the professional and bureaucratic elites of a reinvigorated social democracy will rest their claims to leadership on expertise, not on a sense of pride and obligation. In both the corporation and the state, intelligence has come 'to replace virtue as the acknowledged aim of social life'.[26]

If the intelligent citizen should be prepared to entrust 'control over the allocation of resources and individual freedoms' to the state,[27] the intelligent bourgeois is more likely to place his faith in the market. But in doing so, the self-interested bourgeois is not necessarily turning his back on democracy. On the contrary, by facilitating the free play of market forces, the law promotes the growth and development of capitalist democracy, both at home and abroad. This, according to the law and economics school, has been true ever since the rise of Jacksonian democracy. The movement to replace special charters by general incorporation laws rode a wave of populist hostility towards 'aristocratic privileges' available only to a favoured few. The introduction of limited liability also 'reflects a venerable desire to help out smaller investors, those more typical of the people'. Both legal innovations enabled much wider popular participation in corporate enterprise, thus reflecting the values of 'democracy as much as economics'. But this sort of 'wide participation in businesses that could most advantageously be organised as corporations' depended on 'the limitation of that involvement to the essentially passive act of investment'.[28]

It has been said that 'the corporation is probably a far more democratic mechanism from the viewpoint of shareholders than is government from the point of view of voters'.[29] If so, this is because the shareholder need not display any loyalty to the firm in which he has invested. If he is disappointed in the performance of that corporation he can simply sell out. Nor is he obliged to accept financial, legal or political responsibility for damages or loss that the firm may wrongfully have inflicted on others. To impose unlimited liability on passive investors would discourage individual 'investment in the small firm, or investment by entrepreneurs of modest means'.[30] Democratic capitalism becomes possible, it seems, only when passive investors are able to escape responsibility for or commitment to the joint enterprise to which they have contributed.

If the corporation is purely and simply a capital-raising device, moves to expand the role of shareholders in corporate governance seem likely to injure rather than help shareholders. Fischel claims that 'it is a sham' to promote shareholder democracy 'in the name of either shareholders or of democracy'. Shareholders seeking to maximise the economic return on their investment will generally prefer to 'trust the expertise of professional managers'. Intelligence is more important than civic virtue to the effective governance of the modern business corporation. Corporations are efficient capital-raising devices precisely because they enable 'individuals who have wealth but lack managerial ability to invest while simultaneously allowing professional managers who lack personal wealth to run enterprises'. That being so, Fischel suspects that the real beneficiaries of the corporate governance movement are 'academics, social reformers and regulators who want corporations to sacrifice wealth maximisation in favour of their own notions of moral behaviour'.[31]   On his view, no rational shareholder could ever be tempted to resurrect the republican model of the corporation as a civil body politic.

Indeed, the law and economics movement sometimes denies that the corporation is a real entity at all.   A corporation is one legal manifestation of what economic theory calls a firm.   According to Fischel, firms and markets 'are alternative modes of organising economic activity'.   The firm allows an entrepreneur to avoid some of the costs that would arise if every aspect of the manufacture and sale of a particular good had to be organised through separate exchange transactions in markets for land, labour and capital.   The firm then is nothing more than 'a legal fiction that serves as a nexus for this contracting process' between, inter alia, investors and managers, employers and employees, suppliers and customers.   For Fischel the 'publicly held corporation, therefore, is a type of firm that facilitates the organisation of production which is particularly effective when a large amount of capital is required'.[32]   Conceived as a nexus of contracts, the corporation is denied any organisational or institutional identity of its own.

In its purest form, the inherence doctrine asserts that the corporation is a product of private contract.   Corporate law simply enables entrepreneurs to reduce their agency and transaction costs.   Proponents of this contractual theory of the corporation downplay the mandatory character of the corporate law enforced by the state and its courts.   Pressed to the wall, inherence theorists concede that some provisions of the corporate law constitute the corporation to some limited extent as the creature of the state and not private contract.   Nevertheless, Fischel contends that much 'of corporation law, including fiduciary duties and limitations on distributions for the protection of creditors, can be viewed as standard form contractual provisions that would be negotiated by private contract if not provided by statute'.[33]

It is not immediately obvious why individuals would contract to construct an elaborate political edifice of corporate governance that endows shareholders, but not creditors, bondholders, customers or employers with the right to attend meetings and to vote in elections for boards of directors and on other important corporate decisions.   That governance structure could be understood instead as either the corrupted residue or the embryonic nucleus of a civil body politic.   But inherence theorists refuse analogies between the *polis* and the shareholders meeting.   Nor, they insist, can the role of the shareholder be likened to that of the citizen.   Not even the fact that shareholders possess voting rights justifies analogies between political and corporate government. In the corporate context 'voting rarely serves any function except in extremis'. Given large numbers of widely dispersed shareholders, 'none of the voters has the appropriate incentive to study the firm's affairs and vote intelligently'.[34] Some claim that it 'would make little difference if shareholders, like bondholders, could not vote at all'.[35]

The Economic Interpretation of the Corporate Constitution

But to conclude that there is no good economic reason why shareholders have or exercise votes would be to hand the question over to political or constitutional theory. Voting in corporate law might then be seen as an integral element in a political process of deliberative decision-making. Efforts have been made therefore to demonstrate that shareholder voting can be explained in terms of the distinctive economic function of shareholders, a function that has nothing to do with the powers of reasoned speech essential to those who participate in authority. Shareholders, it is said, really have little or nothing to discuss. Manne insists that there are almost always 'no conflicts in the corporate interests of voting shareholders'.[36] Voting rights exist in the corporation only 'because someone must have the residual power to act (or delegate) when contracts are not complete'. Shareholders, rather than bondholders, managers or employees, get to exercise those rights because they 'are the residual claimants to the firm's income'. Since 'shareholders receive most of the marginal gains and incur most of the marginal costs' associated with new projects, they 'have the right incentives to exercise discretion'. The exercise of discretion through shareholder voting will be consistent and therefore efficient because shareholders 'are a reasonably homogeneous group with respect to their desires for the firm'.[37] They have a shared interest in maximising the economic value of their investment in the firm.

But the assumption of shared interests holds only so long as shareholders are understood not as speaking and acting subjects but rather as surrogates for particular units of capital socialised within a joint enterprise. Having taken on the corporate form, capital becomes a social force of production, 'while the capitalist is reduced to the level of a simple agent, functionary or emissary of this power'.[38] As mere personifications of their capital stake in a corporate enterprise, shareholders do not vote as natural persons appearing before their peers in public. Instead, each individual or institutional shareholder acts 'as the temporary trustee of a piece of paper embodying values to which shareholders and management alike have agreed to adhere in making their "corporate" decisions, whether or not they accept them in their personal lives'. As David Ratner observes, 'management's electorate is not the shareholders but the shares'. It is the shares, not the shareholders, that are homogeneous, with a presumptively common interest in maximising their own value. Along with the one share, one vote rule, 'the institution of voting by proxy, and the use of record dates that result in many votes being cast on behalf of people who are no longer shareholders at the time of the meeting, all combine to depersonalise the decisional powers in corporate elections'.[39]

The one share, one vote rule is a direct affront to the principle of political equality. It operates to entrench the factional interests of large investors. By multiplying the collective action problems faced by the shareholders under any voting regime, the one share, one vote rule permits the plutocratic corruption of the corporate body politic. Fischel denies the republican premise that the principle of one voice, one vote has any place in a 'corporate democracy'. The corporate demos is made up of shares, not shareholders. This regime of corporate governance is the product of private contract. The state could and in the age of special charters often did mandate different voting rules in order to 'serve broader goals than wealth maximisation'. But according to the inherence doctrine 'the optimal voting rules for any particular firm are those that maximise its value'.[40]

The law and economics school teaches that the voting rules for representative governments are not identical to 'the optimal voting rules for publicly held corporations engaged in the production of goods and services'. No one seriously proposes that 'votes in the political arena should be assigned according to wealth'. Conversely, 'there is no reason to believe that principles from political democracy should serve as a model for corporate governance'.[41] That presumptively equal voting rights are attached to shares is a logical consequence of their role in preserving the residual claims of shareholders. Fischel claims that voting rights derive from the shareholders' residual interest in the firm. Along with Easterbrook, Fischel asserts as well that 'each element of the residual interest' should carry an equal voting right. Otherwise, he warns 'there will be a needless agency cost of management'. That last claim assumes that if voting rights were not tied to the extent of property ownership, large investors would have to waste valuable resources persuading other shareholders to give due weight to the overriding goal of wealth maximisation. Because those shareholders 'with disproportionate voting power will not receive shares of the residual gains or losses from new endeavours and arrangements commensurate with their control,' they will be tempted to pursue objectives other than wealth maximisation. In other words, 'they will not make optimal decisions'.[42]

According to the inherence theory, voting rights in the corporation should be left as a matter of private contract, not public law. They exist only to allow decisions to be made that have not already been covered by other contractual terms. If voting rights can be explained wholly in contractual terms, there is no good reason why votes themselves, as distinct from the underlying investment, should not be open to sale and purchase between freely contracting parties.

But at common law shares are freely marketable, voting rights are not. Despite generations of criticism, the policy of the common law remains today 'that the control of stock companies shall be and remain with the holders of the stock. The right to vote is an incident of the ownership of stock, and cannot exist apart from it'. Almost a century ago, Jesse Lilienthal argued that no 'shareholder owes to his fellow shareholders any more of a duty to retain the right to vote upon his own shares, than he does to vote upon them at all, or not to sell, or not to sell them to anyone unworthy'.[43] But the common law refused to accept that there was a fundamental difference between the duties attached to voting rights created by private contract and those established by the public law. In the words of one nineteenth century American court, 'A sale by stockholder of the power to vote upon his shares is illegal for very much the same reason that a sale of his vote by a citizen at the polls, or by a director of a corporation at a meeting of the Board, is illegal'. In every case selling the right to vote 'is a violation of duty; in effect, if not in purpose, a betrayal of trust'.[44] Clearly there is something about the role of the shareholder qua voter that cannot be explained solely in terms of private contract. Even someone as amply endowed with the unimpeachably bourgeois instincts of the corporate raider as T Boone Pickens has been moved to outrage at the corrupt practice of vote selling, describing it as 'un-American' and akin to 'prostitution'.[45]

Diehard defenders of the inherence thesis dismiss such negative reactions to the sale of voting rights. A 'misguided analogy to political democracy', they say, provides no basis for prohibiting that practice, 'or any other voting rule, that has the effect of maximising the value of certain firms'.[46] Others fear the wholesale erosion of shareholder involvement in corporate governance. They insist that shareholders 'should regard the use of their votes as a duty as well as a right'.[47] But what is the nature and scope of that duty? If a shareholder selling his right to vote becomes a whore, what do we call someone who gives his vote away free of charge to a proxy? Membership in a body corporate was once associated with the idea of civic responsibility. Proxy voting has long been deplored as a corruption of the corporate constitution. In the early American republic, one judge noted that voting by proxy might suit the personal convenience of members but it could not 'be for the good of the corporation'. In his view, the 'interest of the company, the good of the public, would be better promoted and more effectively secured by the personal attendance of and mutual interchange of opinions among the members, than by the action of proxies'. If one shareholder votes by proxy, 'they all may, and so the welfare and interest of the company and of the public, be utterly neglected.'[48] Even now, there are those who urge 'abolition of the proxy system altogether'. After all, if general meetings provide regular opportunities to discharge the duty to vote, one is bound to wonder whether it 'would really be too demanding of shareholders to attend if they wish to vote'.[49]

Under the present regime of corporate governance, the answer to that question must be yes. A ban on proxy voting would challenge the basic axioms of received legal and economic theory. Conventional wisdom has it that shareholder preferences are fixed, unitary and homogeneous. All shareholders seek increases in the value of their shares and that is all they seek. So long as most shareholders have confidence that incumbent managers are performing well there is no need to attend the general meeting. Should things go sour, shareholders retain the exit option. Until then, voting rights can be parked safely with managerial or other proxies. In the Anglo-American corporate world, the power of shareholders has been felt more often in the market for corporate control than in the general meeting.

Still, proxy battles at a general meeting do provide an alternative to the market for corporate control for those aiming to take over an established firm. Because voting rights are still attached to shares, they serve as a mechanism through which shareholders can monitor and punish poor managerial performance. All shares may carry voting rights but it is only through the device of proxy voting that they can all be brought into play. The abolition of proxy voting would effectively create a de facto class of non-voting shareholders (as distinct from non-voting shares), most likely leaving the firm in the hands of insiders who control general meetings. We might expect that the end of proxy voting would lead to more frequent judicial interventions into disputes over the oppression of minority shareholders by plutocratic interests using their voting power for improper purposes.[50] Taken on its own, it is not clear what public interest would be served by a ban on voting by proxy.

That being so, both the proxy fight and the takeover tender offer are likely to remain the major options available to corporate raiders challenging incumbent managers. It is true, however, that both strategies are extraordinarily clumsy and expensive ways to deal with managerial inefficiency. All the more so when, as in the United States, legislatures are ready to create or facilitate managerial defences against both hostile takeovers and proxy challenges.[51] Even so, managers who have nothing to fear from a general meeting know that the voting rights of passive investors can be aggregated through the proxy system 'and used to cut down their discretion or even to remove them from office altogether'. Similarly, the market for corporate control exists because, so long as shareholders alone have a vote 'management do not have to take account of anyone else in quite the same way'.[52]

Agency Theory and Corporate Social Responsibility

In the economic interpretation of the corporate constitution, the relationship between managers and owners is one of agency. The residual rights, powers and duties vested in shareholders make them the principals on whose behalf managers strive to maximise profits. But the public corporation has so many widely dispersed shareholders that collective action becomes difficult and costly. The fact that shareholder's views can be ascertained only 'through cumbersome formal procedures makes them suitable only for the crudest kind of decision-making'.[53] For that reason shareholders are not held responsible for the conduct of corporate business. Instead, the power to manage the business is vested by law in a board of directors.

Boards of directors are now subject to a wide range of legal constraints and fiduciary obligations arising from their status as agents of the shareholders. But no one expects managers to be altruists. The law of director's duties assumes that managers will further the interest of the company insofar as it is in their own interest to do so. Most of the reform proposals discussed by those with an interest in corporate governance offer new and improved ways of keeping managerial noses to the grindstone. The ruling assumption is that, when the cat is away, managerial mice will shirk their duties or engage in strategic or opportunistic behaviour designed to feather their own nests at the company's expense. The corporate constitution allows principals to monitor the performance of their agents, if only vicariously, by posting additional watchdogs. Good corporate governance is not an end in itself; it must show up on the bottom line. Whether at a general meeting or while considering his options in the market for corporate control, the 'responsible' investor needs a steady flow of reliable, independently audited information. Under current conditions, there is a clear need for someone independent of management to monitor, evaluate and act upon that flow of information on behalf of all those passive investors who lack the time, energy or resources to overcome the problem of rational apathy. Experience has shown that boards of directors must themselves be monitored to ensure that they serve shareholder rather than managerial interests.

Independent auditors and the appointment of non-executive directors are often touted as solutions to such problems. Other reforms designed to cast the corporate constitution as a monitoring mechanism include changes to liability rules. Shareholders might themselves pay more attention to managerial performance if they were exposed to unlimited liability for corporate wrongdoing, whether tortious or criminal.[54] Once the corporate constitution assumes that economic self-interest is the only reliable predictor of human behaviour, the 'company as an entity capable of being owned disappears from the picture'.[55] As memories of the early modern civil body politic faded, the corporation was reduced to a nexus of contracts. On this model, the firm becomes a mysterious black box operating in an ethical vacuum. The exclusion of ethical concerns in the crafting of corporate constitutions can only be justified on the ground that 'the maximisation of profit on the part of individual enterprises is conducive to the maximisation of wealth of society as a whole'. But that proposition no longer receives universal assent among the leading authorities in the corporate governance movement. Parkinson, for example, rejects 'the argument that companies should be required to maximise their profits because in this way they best serve the public interest'. In his view, 'profit-maximising policies are not always wealth-maximising ones, and even where they are, wealth maximisation may not be the most desirable outcome'.[56]

If maximising corporate profits does not automatically benefit society as a whole, it is no longer obvious why boards of directors should be treated 'as agents exclusively for the shareholders'.[57] Faced with the deficiencies of that 'ideal rule', Parkinson turns to the issue of corporate social responsibility. Even so, he defines corporate social responsibility in economistic terms as the 'uncompensable costs' incurred 'for socially desirable but not legally mandated *action*'. This refers, he adds, 'to *behaviour* that involves voluntarily sacrificing profits, either by incurring additional costs in the course of the company's production processes, or by making transfers to non-shareholder groups out of the surplus thereby generated'. Such 'behaviour' will occur if managers believe that it 'will have consequences superior to those following from a policy of pure profit maximisation'.[58]

Notice Parkinson's elision of the gap between 'action' and 'behaviour'. By treating one as a synonym for the other, Parkinson transforms the meaning of corporate social responsibility. There is a world of difference between responsible behaviour and responsible action. To understand how a corporation might act responsibly one must turn to political philosophy. For Hannah Arendt, in particular, the possibility of political action presupposes the existence of a world held in common. She saw moral agency as the province, not 'of isolated reasoners, but of communal beings'.[59] Economic theory, by contrast, tries to account for the manner in which both corporations and natural persons behave as maximisers of utilities. The law is then pressed into service to modify that behaviour when collective needs clash with individual interests. The major problem posed by the corporate governance movement is the identification of the goals to be achieved by modifying corporate behaviour. The policy choice is between a profit-maximising or a profit-sacrificing version of corporate social responsibility.[60] The need for new forms of corporate *political* responsibility has been all but ignored by expert opinion. The politically responsible corporation would encourage shareholders to transform themselves from passive principals into moral agents free to engage in political action. Such political models of shareholder activism are of little interest to those whose determination to impose properly accountable forms of corporate behaviour leaves little or no public space for deeds and events that deviate from the statistical norm.

Economic Behaviour and Political Freedom

Corporate social responsibility is now described as 'a "process concept", that is, as a concept concerned with the characteristics of the corporate decision-making process and not with particular outcomes'. This process can be understood in two ways depending upon whether one favours a profit-maximising or a profit-sacrificing model of corporate social responsibility. In the first version, 'the reform strategy is to "moralise" the company's decision-making procedures so that its approach resembles that of the responsible individual'. Corporate and individual morality alike become a function of the 'isolated reasoner'. Corporate behaviour is modified 'by factoring an awareness of third-party interests into the decision-making process'. But asking managers to reflect on the consequences for others of corporate projects will not produce anything more than 'modest changes in company behaviour'.[61]

A more ambitious version of corporate social responsibility 'is to make the company more responsive to the interests of affected groups by increasing the ability of those groups to shape corporate conduct'. Corporate behaviour would then be modified by strengthening the ability of such groups 'to impose pressure on the company from the outside or by giving them some constitutional status within the organisation'.[62] Needless to say, neither model of corporate social responsibility requires any of those involved in the decision-making process to renounce their own interest. Instead, corporate responsibility is socialised as institutional investors, non-executive or independent directors serving on audit and remuneration sub-committees of the board, auditors, employees and other stakeholders looking out for themselves all help to monitor managerial performance. Responsibility becomes the built-in, automatic function of a self-regulating system in which managerial conformity to standard operating procedures can usually be taken for granted.

The conformism prescribed by a behaviourist model of corporate governance has its roots in the science of economics. That discipline itself became possible 'only when men had become social beings and unanimously followed certain patterns of behaviour, so that those who did not keep the rules could be considered to be asocial or abnormal'. To the economist, the activities of both owners and managers are best understood as impersonal processes subject to 'the same statistical laws' that 'rule human behaviour and make the multitude behave as it must, no matter how "free" the individual particle may appear to be in its choices'.[63] For its defenders, the nexus of contracts model of the corporation 'is simply an abstraction developed as a useful model for predicting the behaviour of large numbers of people'.[64] The legal regime best calculated to produce predictable corporate behaviour turns, not to the free moral agent, but to the 'external mobilisation of internal self-control resources'.[65] It is difficult to account for responsible political action in the impersonal language of economics and systems theory. Corporate social responsibility demands no more than conformity to the behavioural norms currently governing relations between owners, managers and other stakeholders. Corporate political responsibility demands freedom of action.

Arendt believed that the political realm of freedom must be separated from the economic sphere of necessity. For that reason, she insisted that 'the qualities of the statesman or the political man and the qualities of the manager or the administrator are not only not the same, they very seldom are to be found in the same individual; the one is supposed to know how to deal with men in a field of human relations, whose principle is freedom, and the other must know how to manage things and people in a sphere of life whose principle is necessity'. She feared that to bring 'an element of action into the management of things ... could not but create chaos'. It is the sheer brute force of necessity that ensures 'that the political way of life has never been and will never be the way of life of the many'. The formation of political elites grew out of 'the bitter need of the few to protect ... the island of freedom they have come to inhabit against the surrounding sea of necessity'.[66]

Arendt never appreciated the extent to which islands of conscious corporate power have raised themselves above the level of the multitudes who still behave as they must. To recognise that corporations wield substantial power is not 'to deny the obvious inability and conspicuous lack of interest' among shareholders 'in political matters as such'. It does suggest that the commanding heights of corporate power should be open to those who have 'a taste for public freedom, and cannot be happy without it'. If the public spirited citizen had a rightful place in a public realm of corporate governance, general meetings, like every well-ordered republic, would resemble 'islands in the sea' or 'oases in the desert'.[67] Until that happens the sensible shareholder will steer clear of the 'annual general farce'.[68]

The question is whether public spaces of freedom can or should be constituted within the archipelago of corporate power. There is no doubt that the life of modern civil society depends upon the more or less predictable behaviour of the corporate system. Not many of those involved in a corporate enterprise can hope to experience the joys of public happiness therein. According to Arendt, freedom 'has always been spatially limited'.[69] But that limited space was 'reserved for individuality; it was the only place where men could show who they really and inexchangably were'.[70] That freedom of action 'is possible only among equals'. Equality itself has limitations since 'government of the people by the people' will at best be 'government of the people *by an elite sprung from the people*'.[71] Corporate power could become the modernised vehicle for such an aristocratic form of government. A few among many dispersed shareholders could enjoy the freedom to constitute themselves as a political elite whose members are equally responsible for the conduct of their joint enterprise. Corporate political responsibility must rest upon a natural aristocracy and not the contrived illusion of shareholder democracy. In this aristocratic model of corporate governance, it will not be possible to account for responsibility simply as a non-compensable cost. Owners and managers would discover new opportunities to perform unique deeds and take part in significant events in which the actor has 'constantly to distinguish himself from all others'.[72] If the socially responsible corporation breeds conformity, the politically responsible enterprise will value distinction.

Dual Class Common Stock and the Reinvention of Aristocracy

As it happens, the mysterious workings of the market for corporate control have already created a primitive form of the sort of capital structure that could be used to establish a shareholding aristocracy. We should not be surprised to learn that desperate defenders of shareholder democracy have been among the first to attack dual class common stock. Appeals to the principle of 'corporate democracy' have been raised to resist the issue of shares with differential voting rights or no voting rights at all. Recapitalisations involving different classes of shares, some conveying limited or no voting rights and others with multiple voting entitlements, are becoming more common. This issue recently emerged in Australia when the Murdoch family sought to guarantee its control of News Corporation Ltd through such a dual class recapitalisation of the company's stock. Under this scheme, the insider control group would be issued super voting shares conveying 25 votes each while ordinary shares were limited to a single vote. Like the sale of voting rights, proposals to issue dual class common stock pose fundamental questions about the role of the small shareholder within the publicly listed corporation.   It may be that such developments 'will eventually sound the death knell for corporate democracy'.[73] But such an outcome may not be such a bad thing given the problematic, even illusory, character of what passes for 'shareholder democracy' in the corporate sector. Once corporations are permitted to issue dual class common stock a much more fruitful constitutional analogy to a republican model of the mixed polity becomes both imaginable and desirable.

The response by the corporate governance movement to the problem of dual class capitalisations has not displayed much political imagination. Lame appeals to 'shareholder democracy' combine with worries about possible failures of fiduciary obligations, once managers entrench themselves behind a wall of super voting shares, to generate a renewed faith in the beneficent workings of markets for corporate control and managerial services. Conceding that 'shareholder democracy is more illusory than real,' Jeffrey Gordon has no constitutional alternative to offer. At most, he hopes to stave off an old populist nightmare by declaring 'we need no corporate princes here'. Having lost faith in fickle shareholders and fearing the growth of entrenched corporate fiefdoms, Gordon finds a certain cold comfort in 'the notion that high corporate office is earned and retained on the sufferance of marketplace scrutiny'.[74]

Such a limp and helpless reaction to developments that have such 'profound implications for the corporate balance of power and the market for control' gives cause for concern. If Vivien Goldwasser is right when she claims that the 'issue of differential voting rights ... challenges all the myths, all the historical and legal theories of corporate existence',[75] new opportunities as well as old dangers may be opening up. Thus far, the intellectual leadership of the corporate governance movement has been alive only to the dangers 'of a self-perpetuating managerial elite wielding unaccountable authority over tremendous economic resources'.[76] In the current debate over dual class common stock, the opportunity to challenge the plutocratic premises of the one share, one vote rule will have to be seized by others.

The glib identification of corporate democracy with a rule that attaches equal voting rights to shares rather than to shareholders helps to explain Harry Glasbeek's thinly veiled contempt for the rhetoric of corporate social responsibility. The corporate governance movement remains firmly embedded within the ruling consensus. None of its reform proposals aims to contest the corporate cult of the divine economy. Far from 'attacking the institutions and mechanisms which permit the ruling classes to perpetuate their power', the corporate social responsibility project aims only at raising the consciousness of the ruling elites.[77] Corporate reformers exhort capitalists and managers to behave in a socially responsible manner without reconstituting a corporate body politic wherein the self-regarding bourgeois could learn to speak and act as a public spirited citizen (and vice versa). Proposals to include representatives of various stakeholder constituencies on boards of directors are a poor substitute for a new constitutional order capable of embedding the vast interlocking structure of the corporate economy in a coherent and binding sense of civic purpose. At best, representatives of workers, consumers or creditors can hope that moral suasion will encourage 'responsible' profit-making, while discouraging blatant managerial disregard for other stakeholder interests. But around a table where money still speaks with the loudest voice, managerial performance must conform to the capitalist logic of economic efficiency.

Certainly those who have criticised dual class common stock as an affront to corporate democracy have been careful to articulate their concerns in the language of economic rationalism. Not surprisingly, inherence theorists have mounted a strong counter-attack, contending that dual class stock might help certain firms to maximise their value.[78] The defenders of dual class capitalisation make a more persuasive case than its detractors.[79] It is hardly likely that economic efficiency will suffer unless all publicly listed corporations are required to maintain a one share, one vote regime. But, if differential voting rights are economically rational in certain firms, they may also become a politically dangerous means of concentrating corporate power in ever fewer hands. Not every corporate analogy to political government need be as misguided as the fatuous rhetoric of shareholder democracy. Just as it shows corporate democracy to be an empty slogan, dual class common stock constitutes a new class of shareholders less bedevilled by the collective action problems inherent in the classic Berle and Means corporation. That new class could manifest itself as a self-perpetuating managerial oligarchy dominated by a few corporate princes. In that case, the political character of corporate power would become obvious. But the corporation would hardly become an island of conscious freedom. It would be more apt to become an engine of oppression. At best it will compel us to abandon our individuality 'and acquiesce in a dazed, "tranquilised" functional type of behaviour'. As Arendt pointed out, the 'trouble with modern theories of behaviourism is not that they are wrong but that they could become true'. Those theories reveal 'certain obvious trends in modern society'. The story of the modern business corporation began with 'an unprecedented and promising outburst of human activity'. It may end, as Arendt feared, 'in the deadliest, most sterile passivity history has ever known'.[80] That outcome is not inevitable. Allied to the principle of freedom, dual class common stock could become the formal legal foundation for a new sort of natural aristocracy within the civil constitution of a modern republican society.

Constitutional Choices

The choice facing us is both constitutional and economic in character. It is a matter not just of private contract but also of public law. Critics of dual class capitalisation seek to limit the freedom of investors and managers to enter into voluntary contractual agreements by making the one share, one vote rule mandatory. Unfortunately, the only constitutional principle that is seen to be at stake is the specious doctrine of shareholder democracy. It would make much more constitutional sense to employ dual class shares to distinguish active from passive investors. Small investors and those with no interest in corporate governance could acquire shares with limited or no voting rights. Only natural persons with a significant equity stake in the enterprise would be entitled to voting rights. In a republican model of the dual class corporate polity, voting rights would be attached to shareholders and not to shares. Ideally, each shareholder would have one vote. In particular circumstances, it may be expedient to adopt a regressive voting scheme, merely placing a cap on the voting entitlements of large capital investors. These constitutional arrangements are designed to produce a class of shareholders prepared to accept political responsibility for the governance of a joint enterprise. To preserve the one share, one vote rule within the modern business corporation is to licence the continued abdication by shareholders of that responsibility. After all, under the current regime 'no shareholder, no matter how large his stake, has the right incentives' to monitor the enterprise effectively or to weigh his vote carefully 'unless the stake is 100 per cent'.[81] On the assumption that every shareholder has a fixed preference for enhanced profitability, even the large investor would prefer that others devote their time, energy and resources to achieve that goal on his behalf.

Shareholders actively participating in a dual class model of corporate governance will play a dual role; the good corporate citizen remains a bourgeois investor with a substantial private stake in the enterprise. Passive investors, on the other hand, are under no obligation and have no real opportunity to be anything other than purely self-interested in their behaviour. No dual class corporation that failed to provide an optimal return could hope to raise capital through the issue of non-voting shares. But even coupon clippers may have a social conscience. More private investors might be prepared to enter the share market if they were confident that the uses to which their capital would be put were subject to careful oversight by a self-selecting class of active investors experienced in the art of balancing private and public, individual and corporate interests. No such class of corporate notables can appear unless its members encounter each other as natural persons and political equals. Equality of status need not obtain in other aspects of corporate life so long as it is entrenched in shareholder senates. Only then will the role of the shareholder generate and sustain both a civic sense of commitment to the corporate enterprise and the private satisfactions of enhanced personal wealth.

Nowadays, share ownership has nothing to do with the joys of public happiness. The inherence theorists have demonstrated that the supine shareholder has always been a prominent feature of the corporate landscape. Shareholders have rarely been paragons of civic virtue. Ordinary shareholders 'value votes mostly because they facilitate hostile takeovers' and would probably sell their right to vote if given half a chance. Preoccupied with the return on their investment, they are plainly indifferent to governance issues.   Since most shareholders do not exercise their voting rights, a prohibition of dual class capitalisation rests mainly on the premise that differential voting rights 'reduce the threat of takeovers, and that the operations of the corporate control market are universally beneficial to small shareholders and society'.   But hostile takeovers can have deleterious consequences, not just to stakeholders such as employees and customers, but to shareholders as well.   In fact, 'the threat of the takeover can so reduce the incentive of important shareholders and managers to contribute to the development of the firm that shareholders fare worse than if no takeover threat were operative'.[82]

Even now, the use of dual class common stock may sometimes help to preserve shareholder wealth from the damaging effects of a hostile takeover.   Certainly 'initial public offerings of limited or non-voting stock can never harm investors'.[83]   Investors who value voting rights will simply offer lower prices for securities that carry no such rights.   Dual class re-capitalisations might harm shareholder interests if they serve to insulate incumbent managers from the discipline of the market for corporate control. The point of a dual class structure 'is to fix control of the company in the hands of those who end up holding the class of common stock with superior voting rights'.[84]   But it may actually be efficient for an insider group to retain control by holding 51 per cent of superior voting stock without having to hold 51 per cent of the equity.   A management of family group may simply value control more than outsiders 'and be willing to pay a higher cost for capital in order to secure that control'.   By securing inside control, a dual class capitalisation 'may increase managers' incentives to invest in firm-specific human capital'.   Dual class firms now exhibit highly concentrated ownership of voting rights by managers or families.   Such insider groups may be able to 'overcome collective action problems faced by dispersed shareholders'.[85]   These arrangements provide an alternative monitoring mechanism to the market for corporate control.

Existing dual class firms still attach votes to shares rather than shareholders. The republican model of the dual class corporate polity would divide voting from non-voting shares and endow each holder of a voting share with equal voting rights or, at the very least, place a cap on the votes allowed to large investors.   Would such a regime destroy or substantially impair the capacity of the firm to maximise its value?   As we have seen,[86] the argument against a one voice, one vote rule is that large investors would incur unnecessary agency costs in persuading those with disproportionate voting power to give due weight to the goal of wealth maximisation.   That would be less of a concern in firms where voting shares belonged to an insider group of managers or family members. Even if the costs incurred in a more complex political process of corporate decision-making were higher, there would be countervailing benefits. Decisions would be made in a more considered and reflexive manner. This could be expected to lower the level of risks and other negative externalities imposed upon stakeholders and the wider community.

Substantial shareholders would gain the freedom to act as citizens. No longer could one take the fixed, unitary and homogenous character of shareholder preferences for granted. A bourgeois may be defined 'by *what* his interests are' but the good citizen is recognised by '*how* he has arrived at his choices'. That is why civic action, unlike economic behaviour, is inherently boundless and unpredictable. The good citizen will not only want to act on his choices; he will also 'want to get those choices right'. Shareholder senates based on dual class common stock would encourage and assist the 'potential for critical and conceivably painful self-examination'. Under this regime shareholder preferences would become 'malleable and subject to various kinds of social and political formative mechanisms'.[87] This political possibility is of immense importance if Offe and Preuss are right to claim that 'the role of actors within civil society, both collective and individual, assumes increasing strategic significance for the solution of societal problems'.[88]

To implement a just as well as an efficient system of corporate governance, the law regulating corporate behaviour 'must be complemented at the micro-level of the principled action of conscientious citizens'.[89] The injustice of contemporary corporate law follows from its ineffectiveness. By 'destroying the ethical responsibility of executives who are presumed to be legitimately wholly selfish', the entire monitoring system turns out to be counter-productive. No matter how elaborate and detached the behavioural norms of corporate law become, 'the situational power of company executives whose fundamental orientation is towards the maximisation of their own welfare means that they will always find that law a system of licence'.[90] A political model of corporate law could, however, 'do a great deal either to discourage or to encourage reflexive and deliberative modes of preference learning and preference revision'.[91] A reformed corporate law should therefore create 'institutional arrangements and procedures which could generate selective pressure in favour of this type of reflective and open preference learning, as opposed to fixed preferences that are entirely derivative from situational determinants, rigid beliefs or self-deception'. Reformers should not be unduly concerned that they are abandoning the ideal of shareholder democracy. In the realm of corporate governance, it 'no longer makes sense to ask for broader participation'. What is both necessary and possible is 'a more refined, more deliberative and more reflective formation of the motives and demands ... already in place' among the natural persons who become members of a civil body politic.[92]

But there is no need to impose this republican model on all existing dual class firms or on corporations generally. It would be more useful to experiment with the concept in corporate enterprises whose business has an obvious public service dimension. Media corporations come immediately to mind. Courts have recognised freedom of communication as an essential feature of every functioning representative democracy.[93] In practical terms that freedom belongs to large media corporations, some of them global in their reach, as much as to the ostensibly sovereign people in any given locality. If media corporations have become surrogates and not just vehicles for public opinion, it may not be unreasonable to expect those firms to be governed in accordance with republican principles. So far the courts have not explained how a few autocratic media moguls can be expected to use their freedom from state interference to enhance rather than to corrupt the civic culture of constitutional democracy. Only the creation of a vibrant public sphere within the corporate structures of the infotainment industry will give public opinion a chance to free itself from the insatiable lust for private profits, power and prestige driving today's media empires.

One can easily identify other enterprises that could be reconstituted as civil bodies politic straddling the boundary between private and public. Hospitals, universities and even prisons, along with banks and insurance companies have all fit that description at one time or another. Given the notorious risks to public health and safety associated with their products, tobacco, liquor and gambling interests are plausible candidates for constitutionalisation. Weapons manufacturers and defence industries generally provide other cases where economic efficiency must co-exist with the public interest. It is possible, therefore, to imagine modern business corporations that should strike a balance between constitutional responsibility and private profit. But why do we need such a model? Why should we compromise the ability of the modern business enterprise to effectively perform the utility function that has been its raison d'être? The short answer to that question is that the publicly-listed corporation is not just a pure and peerless model of economic efficiency. Contrary to the inherence doctrine, the corporation is defined, as well, by the political realities of power.

Notes

1   John Dunn, 'The Economic Limits to Politics' in John Dunn, ed, *The Economic Limits to Politics* (Cambridge: Cambridge University Press, 1992) p 30.
2   Quoted in *ibid*, p 30.
3   Benjamin Constant, 'The Liberty of the Ancients Compared with that of the Moderns' in Benjamin Constant, *Political Writings*, ed Biancamaria Fontana (Cambridge: Cambridge University Press, 1988) pp 310-2, 316-7.
4   John Dunn, 'The Identity of the Bourgeois Liberal Republic' in Biancamaria Fontana, ed, *The Invention of the Modern Republic* (Cambridge: Cambridge University Press, 1994) p 207.
5   Dunn, *supra* note 1 at p 31.
6   *Ibid*, p 35.
7   James Willard Hurst, *The Legitimacy of the Business Corporation in the Law of the United States 1780-1970* (Charlottesville: University Press of Virginia, 1970) pp 11, 26, 47.
8   *Ellis v Marshall* (1807) 2 *Mass* 269; *Trustees of Dartmouth College v Woodward* (1819) 17 US 508 (4 Wheaton 514).
9   *Abbott v American Hard Rubber Company* (1861) 33 Barb 578 (NY)
10   Andrew Fraser, *The Spirit of the Laws: Republicanism and the Unfinished Project of Modernity* (Toronto: University of Toronto Press, 1990) pp 194-202.
11   Walter Werner, 'Corporation Law in Search of its Future' (1981) 81 *Columbia Law Review* 1611.
12   *Ibid*, at pp 1614-5.
13   *Liggett Co v Lee* (1933) 288 US 517.
14   Werner, *supra* note 11 at p 1625.
15   Adolf A Berle, Jr and Gardiner C Means, *The Modern Corporation and Private Property* (New York: Macmillan, 1933).
16   Mancur Olson, *The Logic of Collective Action* (Cambridge MA: Harvard University Press, 1971).
17   Lynne L Dallas, 'Two Models of Corporate Governance: Beyond Berle and Means' (1988) 22 *University of Michigan Journal of Law Reform* 19 at p 21.
18   *Ibid*, p 21.
19   Werner, *supra* note 11 at 1630, 1650.
20   *Ibid*, p 1630.
21   *Ibid*, p 1662.
22   Henry G Manne, 'Our Two Corporation Systems: Law and Economics' (1967) 53 *Virginia Law Review* 259 at p 260.
23   H J Glasbeek, 'The Corporate Social Responsibility Movement - The Latest in Maginot Lines to Save Capitalism' (1987) 11 *Dalhousie Law Journal* 359 at p 393.
24   Werner, *supra* note 10; Henry G Manne, 'Mergers and the Market for Corporate Control' (1965) 73 *Journal of Political Economy* 110; Daniel R Fischel, 'The Corporate Governance Movement' (1982) 35 *Vanderbilt Law Review* 1259.
25   Glasbeek, *supra* note 23 at pp 400-1, 366.
26   Christopher Lasch, *The New Radicalism in America, 1889-1963: The Intellectual as a Social Type* (New York: Vintage, 1967) pp 272-3.

27   Glasbeek, *supra* note 23 at p 400.
28   Stephen B Presser, 'Thwarting the Killing of the Corporation: Limited Liability, Democracy and Economics' (1992) 87 *Northwestern University Law Review* 148 at pp 163, 156. Cf Bishop C Hunt, *The Development of the Business Corporation in England 1800-1867* (Cambridge, MA: Harvard University Press, 1936).
29   Henry G Manne, 'Some Theoretical Aspects of Share Voting' (1964) 64 *Columbia Law Review* 1427 at p 1445.
30   Presser, *supra* note 28 at p 164.
31   Fischel, *supra* note 24 at pp 1280, 1276
32   *Ibid*, pp 1261-2.
33   *Ibid*, p 1274.
34   Frank H Easterbrook and Daniel R Fischel, *The Economic Structure of Corporate Law* (Cambridge, MA: Harvard University Press, 1991) p 66.
35   Frank H Easterbrook and Daniel R Fischel, 'Voting in Corporate Law' (1983) 26 *Journal of Law and Economics* 395 at p 397.
36   Manne, *supra* note 29 at p 1441.
37   Easterbrook and Fischel, *supra* note 34 at pp 403-5.
38   Mario Tronti, 'Social Capital', *Telos* 17 (Fall 1973) p 108.
39   David L Ratner, 'The Government of Business Corporations: Critical Reflections on the Rule of "One Share, One Vote"' (1970) 56 *Cornell Law Review* at p 38.
40   Daniel R Fischel, 'Organized Exchanges and the Regulation of Dual Class Common Stock' (1987) 54 *University of Chicago Law Review* 119 at p 141.
41   *Ibid*, p 141.
42   Easterbrook and Fischel, *supra* note 34 at pp 408-9.
43   Jesse W Lilienthal, 'Corporate Voting and Public Policy' (1897) 10 *Harvard Law Review* 428 at pp 428, 438.
44   *Hafer v NY Co*, quoted in *ibid*, p 429.
45   Robert A G Monks and Nell Minow, *Power and Accountability* (New York: Harper, 1991), p 206.
46   Fischel, *supra* note 40 at p 141.
47   Janet Dine, 'The Role of the Non-Executive Director' in Saleem Sheikh and William Rees, *Corporate Governance and Corporate Control* (London: Cavendish, 1995) p 208.
48   *Taylor v Griswold* (1834) 2 Green Rep. (NJ) 223 at p 237.
49   Donald B Butcher, 'The Reform of the General Meetings' in Sheikh and Rees, *supra* note 47 at p 236.
50   Cf *Gambotto v WCP Ltd* (1995) 182 CLR 4332; and Michael J Whincop and Mary E Keyes, 'Corporation, Control, Community: An Analysis of Governance in the Privatisation of Public Enterprise and the Publicisation of Private Corporate Law' (1997) 25 *Federal Law Review* 51.
51   Stephen M Bainbridge, 'Redirecting State Takeover Laws at Proxy Contests' (1992) *Wisconsin Law Review* 1071.
52   Andrew Griffiths, 'Shareholding and the Governance of Public Companies' in Sheikh and Rees, *supra* note 47 at p 61.
53   *Ibid*, at p 67.

54 Cf H Hansmann and R Kraakman, 'Toward Unlimited Shareholder Liability for Corporate Torts' (1991) 100 *Yale Law Journal* 1879.

55 J E Parkinson, *Corporate Power and Responsibility: Issues in the Theory of Company Law* (Oxford: Clarendon Press, 1993) p 178.

56 John Parkinson, 'The Role of "Exit" and "Voice" in Corporate Governance' in Sheikh and Rees, *supra* note 47 at pp 87-89.

57 *Ibid*, p 87.

58 Parkinson, *supra* note 55 at pp 260-261 (emphasis added).

59 Jeffrey C Isaac, *Arendt, Camus and Modern Rebellion* (New Haven: Yale University Press, 1992) p 114.

60 Parkinson, *supra* note 55 at p 261.

61 *Ibid*, pp 344-346.

62 *Ibid*, p 346.

63 Hannah Arendt, *The Human Condition* (Chicago: University of Chicago Press, 1958) pp 42, 323.

64 Stephen M Bainbridge, 'Community and Statism: A Conservative Contractarian Critique of Progressive Corporate Law Scholarship' (1997) 82 *Cornell Law Review* 101 at p 119.

65 Gunther Teubner, 'Corporate Fiduciary Duties and Their Beneficiaries: A Functional Approach to the Legal Institutionalisation of Corporate Responsibility' in K J Hopt and G Teubner, eds, *Corporate Governance and Director's Liabilities* (Berlin: Walter de Gruyter, 1985).

66 Hannah Arendt, *On Revolution* (Harmondsworth: Penguin, 1973) pp 274-276.

67 *Ibid*, pp 277-279.

68 Butcher, *supra* note 49 at p 229.

69 Arendt, *supra* note 66 at p 275.

70 Arendt, *supra* note 63 at p 41.

71 Arendt, *supra* note 66 at pp 275-277.

72 Arendt, *supra* note 63 at p 41.

73 Vivien R Goldwasser, 'Differential Voting Rights and the Super Share–In Search of an Accommodation on the Merits' (1994) 7 *Corporate and Business Law Journal* 205 at p 205, 241.

74 Jeffrey N Gordon, 'Ties that Bond: Dual Class Common Stock and the Problem of Shareholder Choice' (1988) 76 *California Law Review* 1 at p 78.

75 Goldwasser, *supra* note 73 at p 241.

76 Gordon, *supra* note 74 at p 78.

77 Glasbeek, *supra* note 23 at p 400.

78 Fischel, *supra* note 40; Peter L Swan and Gerald Garvey, 'Response to the Australian Stock Exchange's Discussion Paper on Appropriate Voting Rights for Equity Securities' (1991) 9 *Company and Securities Law Journal* 158.

79 Joel Seligman mounts a sustained attack on dual class capitalisations in 'Equal Protection in Shareholder Voting Rights: The One Common Share, One Vote Controversy' (1986) 54 *George Washington Law Review* 1. See also, Saul Fridman, 'Super-Voting Shares: What's All the Fuss About?' (1995) 13 *Company and Securities Law Journal* 31.

80 Arendt, *supra* note 63 at p 322.

81   Easterbrook and Fischel, *supra* note 34 at p 67.

82   Swan and Garvey, *supra* note 78 at pp 160, 168.

83   Fischel, *supra* note 40 at p 147.

84   Ronald J Gilson, 'Evaluating Dual Class Common Stock: The Relevance of Substitutes' (1987) 73 *Virginia Law Review* 807 at p 811.

85   Fischel, *supra* note 40 at pp 137, 144.

86   Easterbrook and Fischel, *supra* text accompanying note 42.

87   Claus Offe, 'Micro-Aspects of Democratic Theory: What Makes for the Deliberative Competence of Citizens?' in Axel Hadenius, ed, *Democracy's Victory and Places* (Cambridge: Cambridge University Press, 1997) pp 81-104.

88   Claus Offe and Ulrich K Preuss, 'Democratic Institutions and Moral Resources' in David Held, ed, *Political Theory Today* (Oxford: Polity, 1991) p 166.

89   *Ibid*, p 166.

90   David Campbell, 'The Role of Monitoring and Morality in Corporate Law: A Criticism of the Direction of Present Regulation' (1997) 7 *Australian Journal of Corporate Law* 343.

91   Offe and Preuss, *supra* note 88 at p 170.

92   *Ibid* at p 168.

93   *Australian Capital Television v The Commonwealth* (1992) 66 ALJR 695.

3 Corporations and the Political Realities of Power

Introduction

There are two principal ways of demonstrating that the modern business corporation is governed not just by the economic logic of efficiency but also by the political realities of power. One approach is to examine the *external* political forces shaping corporate law. In every Western nation-state, corporate governance has been an important matter of political debate and decision. Not every organisational form that might be available in a perfect capital market will receive the necessary political backing from the state. Some will become the object of intense public opposition. Corporation and securities law does not simply facilitate private contractual undertakings. Rather, the law favours some forms of joint enterprise and forbids others. Legally prescribed forms of business organisation may also be suitable for a firm at one stage of its development and not at another. It is difficult to deny, therefore, that the legal regime governing the corporate sector is the product of political as well as economic influences.

In economic theory, every firm goes through a definite life cycle. Companies born with 'low market shares in fast growing industries require a great deal of cash to increase their market shares'. Because the future of such firms is uncertain, they are called 'question marks'. Should such companies 'succeed in increasing their market share they become stars; if they fail they become dogs'. Once a company achieves a high share of a slow-growing market it produces cash and requires little outside capital. Such firms are known as 'cash cows'.[1] At different stages in a firm's life cycle, changes in corporate governance arrangements might introduce new sources of efficiency. The governance rules that promote optimal performance in a 'question mark' firm may produce dysfunctions in a 'cash cow'. Politics may intervene, however, to prevent a shift to a more efficient governance regime. On a contractarian analysis, politics intrudes into the realm of economic efficiency to expand or reduce the range of legally permissible organisational designs. But in a perfect capital market the choice between governance options would be free of that alien influence.

If the choice between competing corporate regimes were dictated solely by the economic logic of efficiency in a perfect market with no transaction costs, there would be no need to reconstitute the corporation as a civil body politic. *Homo economicus* would expel *homo politicus* from the body corporate. But, in our imperfect world, politics remains central to the *internal* life of the corporate sector as well. This is not just because the visible hand of managerial power has a firm grip on the modern business enterprise. Politics is also involved in the distribution of power resources among other players within the corporate entity. At every stage of its life cycle every firm develops its own internal political order. Every firm operates within a political environment. Every firm also possesses its own distinctive political culture, be it plutocratic, autocratic, oligarchic or perhaps even democratic. Simply by associating together in a joint enterprise, the combination of interests in the corporate entity generates new sources of political power. That power is not always subservient to market forces. Nor is it the case that only managers seek to usurp the authority that properly belongs to the shareholding owners of the publicly listed corporation. Other stakeholders, such as employees, suppliers, creditors and customers may demonstrate their own variable capacity to affect the process of corporate decision-making. However it may be distributed within particular firms, there is no doubt that the managerial, professional and propertied elites who control the corporate sector wield significant political power.[2]

Corporate power can be organised and exercised in more than one way. There are alternatives to the standard Berle-Means corporation with its strong managers and weak owners. In some countries, the American pattern of dispersed shareholders and centralised managerial control has never corresponded to the organisational realities of corporate enterprise.[3] Even in the United States, prominent business writers have begun to speak of the 'eclipse' and the 'obsolescence' of the public corporation, while promoting other, allegedly more efficient, models of corporate governance.[4] If past experience is any guide, the search for alternatives to the public corporation will probably encounter stiff opposition from constituencies inside as well as outside the corporate sector.

Dual class capitalisations offer one alternative to the dominant model of corporate organisation. Opposition to the dual class firm usually invokes the shopworn slogan of corporate democracy. In an existing company, the point of a dual class recapitalisation would be 'to reduce the voting power of its existing public shareholders'.[5] No longer would all shares carry one vote. Rather some shares would enjoy multiple voting rights. Political resistance to such schemes has sought to bolster the commitment of both stock exchanges and regulatory bodies to the one share, one vote rule.

That defensive strategy may be circumvented by corporate insiders who alter the form of the transaction to accomplish the same result. The dual class capitalisation is not the only way to fix control in an individual or group already possessed of a substantial stake in the company. The leveraged buy out (LBO) is another method by which a putatively 'democratic' regime of corporate governance can be reconstituted as a managerial or family oligarchy. Both the dual class capitalisation and the LBO aim 'to shift control to management or an existing shareholder group'.[6] The justification for both strategies is identical: centralising control in an insider group of active investors will increase the value of the company and its shares. That economic rationale for these control transactions remains largely oblivious to the political implications of the choice between these and other models of corporate governance. The shift away from the Berle-Means corporation towards novel capital structures that thoroughly recast relationships between investors, managers and other stakeholders is fraught with political dangers. There is already good reason to wonder whether the simple constitutional forms of the bourgeois liberal republic can cope with the new globalised forms of concentrated corporate power.

The Politics of Corporate Finance

The apparent novelty of the language employed in the brave new world of dual class capitalisations and leveraged buy-outs can be misleading. By comparison with the passive shareholders made notorious by Berle and Means, the active investors engineering LBO partnerships represent a sharp break with tradition. But on closer examination, it seems that we are confronted with the return of the repressed. Dual class transactions, LBOs and the activist movement among institutional investors all point to the renewed power of finance capital in business life. Jensen observed that 'LBO partnerships and merchant banks are rediscovering the role played by active investors prior to 1940 when Wall Street banks such as J P Morgan & Company were directly involved in the strategy and governance of the public companies they helped create.'[7] In those days, the highly visible power of finance capital provoked a strong populist backlash.

A series of populist laws and regulations caused Morgan's model of investor activism to fade away for a time. But Jensen claims that the long-term effect of those restrictions on insiders and banks 'has been to insulate management from effective monitoring and to set the stage for the eclipse of the public corporation'.[8] If LBO partnerships and dual class transactions are indeed the wave of the future, it is already clear that inefficient managers will not be the only group to feel the sting of the discipline to be imposed by the global emissaries of a resurgent finance capital. It may be that the stage is being set for another round in the perennial struggle between the people and the financial interests. Populist rumblings could be heard in the late 1980s when concern mounted over the huge burden of corporate debt left behind after the takeover boom of the previous few years. As if to still populist fears, Jensen assured his readers that this mountain of debt was actually a blessing in disguise. Despite appearances, 'the leveraging of corporate America has helped to overcome the central weakness of the public corporation - the conflict between owners and managers over the control and use of corporate resources'.[9]

Jensen flatly denies that the public corporation is an inherently efficient organisational form. In fact, he suggests that the 'public corporation is not suitable in industries where long-term growth is slow, where internally generated funds outstrip the opportunities to invest them profitably or where downsizing is the most productive long-term strategy'.[10] Shareholders often find it impossible to force management to disgorge the massive surpluses these cash cows generate. In the late 1980s, Ford was sitting on fifteen billion dollars in cash and securities. The public corporation is hugely wasteful and inefficient despite all the business propaganda to the contrary. Just how wasteful and inefficient can be seen in the large premiums of up to 40 per cent and 50 per cent that shareholders have received in takeover transactions.[11]

When Jensen preaches the gospel of efficiency, he endows finance capital with a providential mission in the growth of the divine economy. The pitch is simple: the substitution of debt for equity leads to large efficiency gains. In his view, the cash cow is an inefficient producer of wealth. It would be more efficient to distribute cash surpluses to shareholders, allowing them to seek the most profitable investment outlets. By restructuring equity as debt, it is possible to achieve the same result. After a typical LBO, debt has become 'in effect a substitute for dividends - a mechanism to force managers to disgorge cash rather than spend it on empire-building projects with low or negative returns, bloated staffs, indulgent perquisites and organisational inefficiencies'. In the case of dividends, management has a discretion whether or not to pay out cash flows. 'Borrowing allows no such managerial discretion.' For that reason, 'a company's creditors wield far more power over managers than its public shareholders'.[12]

Jensen celebrates the role of debt as 'a powerful agent for change'.[13] Certainly there can be little doubt that capital markets are changing enormously. Not only can debt be substituted for equity in the capital structure of the corporation, but the equity holdings themselves can be privatised. Public equity is being steadily replaced by large 'private positions' and debt.[14] The resurgent power of finance capital is also manifest in the proliferation of large institutional investors. Not surprisingly, institutional investors loom very large in the financing of the LBO Associations that Jensen locates at the cutting edge of organisational innovation. Institutional investors are a major source of equity capital. Banks, insurance companies, superannuation and mutual funds are now encouraged by corporate reformers to become active investors, if not necessarily in the grand manner epitomised by the House of Morgan in the baronial era of finance capital.[15]

Whether their influence is felt through debt or through equity financing, institutional investors could become significant actors in corporate governance. There is no shortage of voices urging the great financial institutions to assume such a role. Jensen is not the only prominent business writer to deplore the inefficiency of the present system of accountability to public shareholders. That increasingly widespread concern has emboldened some corporate reformers to advance proposals that would have been the stuff of populist nightmares a few decades ago.

Nowadays the literature on corporate governance reflects the dominant assumption that the public interest in corporate governance is best served when the firm pursues the single goal of maximising its own financial value. By straying from that objective, the public corporation has fallen into disrepute. It is now held up by many as an organisational pathology to be avoided. But expert help is at hand. The power of high finance now presents itself in a therapeutic role. 'Healthy corporations', we are told, 'need long-term commitment from involved owners'.[16] A 'healthy system' of corporate governance depends upon the accountability of managers to owners. This requires not only the appropriate sort of long-term shareholders but also relationships of trust and mutual confidence. By helping managers to keep their eye on the ball, institutional investors will enhance corporate performance. Or so it is hoped. Monks and Minow, for example, believe the solution lies in 'accountability to a category of "permanent" shareholders' such as the great commercial banks in Germany. The Japanese system of corporate cross-ownership serves much the same function. In this view,

'Management needs to be made accountable to someone who has the power, the motive, the perspective and the ability to represent the public interest effectively'. Monks and Minow have no doubt that 'institutional investors, particularly the pension funds, can play that role'.[17]

A critical response to such proposals can take two forms: the one practical, the other principled. On the practical level, it can be shown that 'institutional investors, and particularly those agents that run them, have insufficient interest' or incentive to become active monitors of managerial performance.[18] The other, principled, response is to argue that this new modelled corporatist strategy should not even be tried. Opposition to the fusion of finance and industrial capital could be based upon either populist or republican grounds. Whatever the differences between those perspectives, both would deny finance capital the power to act as the virtual representative of society as a whole. Certainly a more active role in corporate governance for the institutional overlords of the capital markets would require the deliberate deconstruction of the populist legacy in Anglo-American law and political culture.

On the other hand, perhaps populists have no cause for concern. There are good reasons to doubt whether top managers in large, impersonal and bureaucratic institutional investors aspire to become the lords of creation as their predecessors on Wall Street once seemed to be.[19] It is true that the increased concentration of shareholding among institutional investors makes shareholder activism more rational. It is also true that 'institutional shareholders are hobbled by a complex web of legal rules that make it difficult to own large percentage stakes or undertake joint efforts'.[20] But the loosening of those legal restraints would not necessarily lead institutional investors to discipline corporate managers in the interests of all shareholders.

Shareholder activism has become feasible under the current governance regime only because of the vast increase in institutional ownership. Large individual shareholders have substantial incentives to become active investors when they have an increased stake in outcomes, so that there is an 'increased probability that their vote will affect the outcome' and when coordinated voting among large shareholders becomes easier.[21] But institutional investors may not behave as if they are individual shareholders. Institutional investors are agents, not principals. As Edward Rock demonstrates, the potential divergence of interests between principals and agents threatens the collective action gains that might otherwise flow from an increased concentration of shareholding.[22]

Rock contends 'that there are precious few incentives for money managers to act in the interests of their principals'. One should never 'assume that agents will act like principals'. Even if improved corporate governance does 'increase the value of managed portfolios, it does not follow that improving corporate governance will be in the interests of the money managers'. If 'money managers are evaluated in comparison to other managers and market indices', they 'will have no selective incentives to engage in actions that improve the performance of widely diversified funds across the board'. They also face significant disincentives in that corporate governance activities are costly. Whenever competition between portfolio managers leads to cost-cutting pressures, shareholder activism will become a needless luxury. Rock notes that the actual manifestations of institutional shareholder activism have 'been uneven, episodic and trendy'. Experience, he suggests, does 'not unambiguously support an optimistic scenario'. Institutional investors have had a modest success in organising campaigns against takeover defences. But this reflects their desire to preserve a premium for exiting during a takeover transaction. What 'shareholders are willing to do to preserve their ability to exit says little about what they can or will do with respect to disciplining management'.[23]

But what if Rock's scepticism turns out to be misplaced? Once institutional investors acquire the capacity to monitor and discipline corporate managers, the concentrated power of finance capital will become the virtual representative, not just of shareholders, but of society at large. Because the public interest in corporate governance is conventionally identified purely and simply with increases in shareholder wealth, money managers will serve society best by aiming to maximise the value of their own corporate shareholdings. What is good for the pension funds will, by definition, be good not just for General Motors but for the entire McWorld colonised by the corporate monoculture. If collective action problems undermine a productive system of corporate governance, the orthodox 'solution is the undiluted fiduciary obligation of corporate managers and directors to shareholders who are themselves fiduciaries - the institutions'.[24]

The Populist Fragmentation of Finance Capital

As things stand now, 'American managers owe fiduciary duties to an abstraction, a faceless stock market'. That state of affairs has led Mark Roe to conclude: 'Personification could improve performance. Loyalty to real people may motivate better than legally mandated loyalty to an abstraction'.[25] Following that logic, the German and Japanese models of institutional ownership are often held up as desirable alternatives to the American pattern of dispersed shareholders and unaccountable managers. In both Germany and Japan, 'permanent' shareholders exercise control over major enterprises. Because the 'permanent' owners maintain close surveillance over operations corporate management can be held accountable. German 'universal banks own up to 20 per cent of the total of outstanding capital' and 'also vote enough proxies to be able to exercise voting control at shareholder meetings'. In Japan companies are 'owned' by their customers and suppliers. The resulting industrial groupings involve an 'intensive interrelationship' that fosters 'mutual dependency and accountability'.[26]

Poor governance, it is said, has affected adversely the competitive performance of American corporations.[27]   Better forms of corporate governance could help to eliminate the mounting costs of poor management. But shifting to a different model of corporate governance is easier said than done. The difficulties, moreover, are not simply economic or technological in character.   Indeed, the very existence of marked divergences between German, Japanese and American corporate structures and capital markets suggests that Werner's inherence thesis[28] is badly flawed. Most American scholars have taken it for granted that the corporation is a legal instrument designed only 'to provide firm central direction for the enterprising use of pooled assets'. The American business corporation emerged, therefore, as the more or less inevitable response to economic and technological forces. On this reading of corporate history, the separation of ownership and control was implicit in the economic utility of the corporate device. Investors were assured 'that they had a vehicle for limiting their investments of time and energy as well as of money'. It was the inherent 'combination of firm direction and limited commitment' that supposedly made the corporation such 'an attractive instrument for business'.[29]   But that American model of corporate governance has not been attractive to German or Japanese business. Nor has the German and Japanese disinclination to adopt the American model prevented their economic success.

A comparative examination of American, German and Japanese corporate history suggests an alternative to the inherence thesis. According to Mark Roe, the development of the modern American business corporation 'is not just the result of efficiency-driven economic evolution'. On the contrary, corporate structure is 'also the result of American politics, particularly the politics that influenced and often dictated the way financial intermediaries - banks, insurers, pension funds and mutual funds - moved savings from households to firms'. Far from being inherent in the very nature of the modern business corporation, the separation of ownership from corporate control was the product of a deliberate political campaign to fragment the power of financial intermediaries. In place of the inherence doctrine, Roe emphasises the political fragmentation of corporate control. On his reading of the legal history of the corporation, 'American politics repeatedly prevented financial intermediaries from becoming big enough to take influential big blocks of stock in the largest enterprises'. Given a pattern of large-block stockholding, 'corporate authority would differ from what it is now, because owners with big blocks of stock can influence managers'.[30]

Werner's inherence thesis fails to recognise the extent to which the politics of corporate governance has been shaped by the powerful traditions of American populism. Roe defines populism as 'a widespread attitude that large institutions and accumulations of centralised economic power are inherently undesirable and should be reduced, even if concentration is productive'. Antitrust law has obviously been inspired by populist politics but so too were the 'rules governing the range and size of financial institutions and their influence in corporate governance'. Interest group politics also played an important role in corporate legal history as small-town bankers and managers both joined in the political struggle to fragment the power of large financial institutions.[31]

Roe himself is no populist. On the contrary, he believes that populism has probably slowed down the competitive adaptation of American business by foreclosing other possible and desirable forms of corporate governance. Roe favours more 'competition among governance systems' but recognises that the powerful populist strain in American political culture will make it difficult to overcome 'the country's history of financial fragmentation'. Any move to create powerful financial intermediaries on the German model will require political action. In Germany and Japan, no less than in the United States, politics has shaped the structure of the big business corporation. The corporation is everywhere 'bound to a political culture and cannot be understood as solely an economic, transaction - cost - reducing organisation'. The firm, wherever it is located, 'must not only be effective economically, but fit politically'.[32] If new forms of institutional shareholder activism develop in the United States, one might conclude that the long-standing populist hostility to finance capital is no longer a potent political force. But, given the deep-rooted popular suspicion of concentrated private economic power, increased levels of shareholder activism among money managers may well provoke political opposition.

The risk of such a populist backlash does not discourage Roe. He remains convinced that the agency costs plaguing the relationship between owners and managers could be significantly reduced by enhancing the power of financial institutions. But existing populist laws and regulations will impede the search for alternative financial and organisational forms. That being so, 'efforts to resolve the agency problem with outside financial control must somehow defeat or elude the political restrictions'. In Roe's judgement, the prospects of overcoming the populist legacy are not altogether bleak: 'while institutions in the 1990s still have a couple of strikes against them in the political arena, they do not *have* to lose the political battle'.[33]

Whether the forces of finance capital *should* emerge triumphant in a political struggle to control the corporate sector is another question. Given present trends, financial intermediaries might come to exercise corporate control through *private* equity and debt, thereby reducing the already vestigial forms of the corporate public sphere to a practical nullity. Faced with such dangers, populism has little or nothing new to offer. The populist's only hope is that the rational apathy of the money managers will match that of widely dispersed individual shareholders. But the danger remains that, under certain circumstances, institutions might replace their present preference for liquidity with a strong interest in corporate control. In those circumstances, we can be confident that 'the dark side of relational investing' will pose persistent problems.[34]

With their continuing commitment to a particular firm, relational investors are generally portrayed in a positive light. Less prone to take a Wall Street walk when the going gets tough, the relational investor takes a greater interest in control and governance issues. Institutional investors such as banks, pension funds, insurance companies, mutual funds and the like have been touted as the white knights of shareholder democracy. But we have seen that Edward Rock suggests that money managers 'lack significant positive economic incentives to protect shareholders' interests' while facing 'significant disincentives'.[35] Partly for that reason, this season's candidate for shareholders' champion is the more inclusive category of relational investors.[36] Firms outside the financial services sector may also develop long-term relationships with one another. The ideal relational investor would be an individual or firm with both the ability to discipline management and economic interests aligned with those of other stockholders.[37]

Rock acknowledges that relational investing may sometimes have a positive influence on corporate performance. But things can go wrong. Relational investing also has the potential to corrupt the corporate sector. In one scenario it may happen that 'an investor acquires a large (for example, 9.5 per cent) interest in a firm at a discount in exchange for protecting incumbent managers from displacement or, more generally, from threats to their autonomy'. While the relational investor may profit from protection money, the other shareholders will lose. Another sort of corporate corruption arises when a 'relational investor uses its substantial investment, not to protect managers or improve management, but to advance its own business, i.e. by securing favourable contracts with the firm'. Rock fears that 'profiting from protection payments, when offered, or expanded sales or increased margins will dominate good relational investing'. After all, the public-spirited relational investor 'will only receive a pro rata share of the gains from improved management' while it will receive *all* of the protection money and *all* of the profits from increased sales or increased profit margins.[38]

Not only does the relational investor have to bear the full cost of improving management, the gains to be expected from disciplining managers 'are far more speculative than gains from either a protection payment, expanded sales or increased margins'. Owing to the divergent interests among shareholders, managers and relational investors, the growth of relational investment is a worrisome development. Rock provides a sober analysis of the positive incentives favouring corrupt conduct among relational investors. The problem is a simple one: 'a virtuous relational investor only benefits pro rata while a corrupt relational investor receives 100 per cent of any direct or indirect payoffs'. Since existing legal approaches encourage the 'good relational investor's rational apathy and the bad investor's temptation', corporate law is ill-equipped to control corrupt relational investment.[39] In seeking to reform the relationship between corporate finance and corporate governance, we should avoid the simplistic solutions often associated with the paranoid style (however democratic the promise) of populist politics.[40]

In American history, the populist imagination has been easily inflamed by the spectre of a financial octopus controlling the productive energies of ordinary workers and businessmen.[41] But once government acted to curb the 'parasitic', outside financial control of productive enterprise, populists posed no challenge to the managerial revolution in corporate governance.[42] This time around, finance capital will be offering to rescue us from the wasteful, inefficient public corporations now sheltering under legal restrictions imposed in a politically primitive populist era. By fragmenting finance, populism forced the owner's power to shift elsewhere. Partly by default, control shifted to managers. Because 'the American public would not permit large, powerful financial institutions that would share power at the top', the direction of large corporations was 'further centralised in manager's hands. Managers may not be political heroes to the average voter, but they are dispersed'. That 'makes them less visible targets than financial institutions'.[43] In effect, populist laws and regulations have helped to entrench the managerial elite that has brought the large public corporation to the brink of obsolescence.   Lacking any political theory of corporate governance, populists may be forced to bend the knee to the restored reign of finance capital. Certainly no one believes any longer that the threadbare slogan of shareholder democracy offers a real alternative to managerialism. As a consequence, academic writers on corporate governance confess themselves unable to do anything more than potter 'around the margins, seeking to understand, and perhaps thereby to shift slightly the balance between vice and virtue'.[44]

Accountability versus Responsibility

Political theory is a normative enterprise. It does not emerge spontaneously from the political history of corporate finance. To demonstrate that the structure of corporate ownership and control is moulded by the political, as well as the economic environment of the firm does not require any commitment to the corporation as a civil body politic. At most, it suggests that politics impinges on the corporation from the outside. Looking from the inside out, it remains possible to conceive the corporation as a more or less efficient nexus of contracts. Roe's political model of corporate finance is consistent with the view that society itself is a nexus of contracts. But the existence of contracts does not imply the absence of politics. In 'a broad-based democracy, not all contracts will survive'. The power of finance capital is based on contractual arrangements between suppliers and users of equity investments. But if enough people dislike 'powerful private financial institutions, politics will, all else being equal, ban them'.[45] The result may be the survival of other less efficient contracts, such as those constituting the public corporation. If there is no effective competition among governance systems, waste and inefficiency will begin to undermine corporate performance. On this model, autonomous managerial power, or politics more generally, has the chance to root itself in the corporate culture only under conditions of imperfect competition among governance regimes. In a perfect market, every firm could effortlessly select the ownership structure that would maximise corporate value at any given stage in its life cycle. But the parties contracting for a particular set of governance arrangements would be aiming to satisfy their needs as *bourgeois,* not as *citizens.* Corporations constituted as a civil bodies politic are not the product of private bargains struck in the markets for products, services and corporate control. A political theory of corporate governance would be based not on a nexus of contracts, but on the urgent need for a new covenant uniting rulers and ruled.

Corporate governance is generally conceived as a problem of accountability. But that has not made it a political matter. Corporate accountability has to do with the economic performance of agents. The institutional investors to whom managers are to be made accountable are not expected to act as citizens. At best, they serve as watchdogs. At worst, they turn out to be watchdogs that flee at the first sign of trouble. Monks and Minow associate accountability with a restoration of trust between investors and managers.[46] In fact, the relationship between managers and their institutional watchdogs is more likely to be based on passive distrust. Accountability has to do with reciprocal control. Managers and financial intermediaries are both accountable to shareholders, but they are not identical with that body. Managers and institutional investors, alike, are representatives, fiduciaries or agents of shareholders too passive or too preoccupied to be watchdogs. According to Benjamin Barber, the 'chief device of accountability is representation itself, an institution that permits public watchdogs to spend most of their time pursuing their private business while functionaries and hirelings (delegates and representatives) minister to the public business'.[47] When institutional investors take on the job of disciplining managers, the notional responsibility of shareholder principals is finally dissolved into the accountability of one set of managerial agents to another. To whom shareholders are accountable for renouncing the responsibilities of ownership remains unclear.

In the ruling ideology of corporate governance, the legitimacy of the modern business corporation depends, first and foremost, upon its economic utility. The first, if not the only, responsibility of every firm to society is to maximise its own wealth.[48] All shareholders, large and small, are presumed to have a common interest in the 'efficient' management of corporate assets and opportunities. Politics is often portrayed as a process of resolving conflicts among competing interests and divergent principles. Politics has to do with power, not efficiency. Given the assumed one interest of all shareholders, politics has no obvious role to play in corporate governance. In the orthodox view, politics is the organisational grime that gums up the works when the watchdog goes to sleep. Accountability is a device employed to keep the corporate machine clean, lean and mean.

A republican model of the corporation requires not just individual accountability but also civic responsibility. It assumes that politics is a necessary and desirable feature of life in any joint enterprise. In place of the passive distrust characteristic of the watchdog, the creation of a common civic identity among responsible members of the corporate body politic will promote 'reciprocal empathy and mutual respect'.[49] We need to consider republican alternatives to the 'remorganisation'[50] of the economy because the corporation is not simply a private unit of capital accumulation operating in an alien political environment. Like it or not, the modern business corporation is a body politic. The choice to be made among the alternatives to the publicly-listed corporation is political as well as economic in its nature and consequences.

The political styles of corporate governance may take several forms. We have already contrasted the passive distrust associated with the quest for managerial accountability to the civic bonds of empathy, mutual respect and shared responsibility that could emerge within a corporation constituted as a little republic. For those trapped within a corporate tyranny, reciprocal fear and mutual contempt are more likely to be the norm. Even under the most benevolent managerial regime, shareholders cannot trust themselves to play a significant role in the direction of corporate business. Only by delegating an absolute discretion to management to run the business is it possible to avoid the 'pathologies that would emerge in the strategies of shareholder voting'. Even in the judgement of defenders of 'shareholder democracy' such as Jeffrey Gordon, 'shareholder initiative would produce strategic behaviour designed to maximise private gains at the expense of common gains'. These pathologies, he believes, can only be avoided by setting management up as a 'term-limited dictatorship to avoid the economic losses of inconsistent choices that would result from shareholder voting'.[51] Outside financial control of corporate enterprise need not be either dictatorial or tyrannical. But nor should such arrangements be portrayed simply as a technical device to enhance productive efficiency.

Every governance regime reflects the distribution and exercise of political power within a complex social organisation. It is to the internal organisation of the corporation that accountability theorists turn when things go wrong. When corporations commit crimes, shareholders are not likely to bear responsibility. Nor will the great mass of passive investors be inclined to hold managers or other employees accountable for unlawful behaviour. Instead, Brent Fisse and John Braithwaite believe that corporate managers should be legally compelled to deal with criminal behaviour through their own internal corporate justice systems. Such a private process of self-investigation would be required to fully identify 'the responsible corporate policies, technologies, management systems, and decision-makers' while coming 'up with a plan of remedial action, disciplinary action and compensation to victims'. At present, individual accountability 'is more the exception than the rule in the context of offences committed on behalf of large-scale organisations'. In fact, the 'way in which legal liability is structured today often confers a de facto immunity on corporate managers, who are typically shielded by a corporate entity which takes the rap'.[52] But, in the context of criminal liability, the corporation is separate from both owners and managers. It becomes little more than 'an ingenious device for the maximisation of profit and the minimisation of responsibility'.[53] Under these circumstances, it is not clear how corporate managers could be induced to prosecute unlawful behaviour through an internal justice system. By galvanising the corporate body politic into action, an authoritative body of active shareholders could overcome the force of institutional inertia, endowing internal justice systems with the power to reshape corporate behaviour. But in the absence of owners (principals) responsible for the behaviour of their agents, only the legal authority of the democratic nation-state remains to counterbalance the unaccountable power of the managerial overclass.

Fisse and Braithwaite believe that private justice systems could be forced to act if offending firms were exposed to the ultimate legal sanction of corporate capital punishment. In their view, 'the law should hold an axe over the head of a corporation that has committed the *actus reus* of a criminal offence'. The axe would take the form of 'liquidation, withdrawal of the licence or charter of the firm to operate'.[54] It remains to be seen whether judges and regulators could ever summon the political will to wield that axe. Corporate managers have a demonstrated capacity to erect a defensive shield around their own domain. The big business corporation produces political power as well as profits. Those political resources have so far been successfully displayed to deflect responsibility for criminal behaviour away from particular corporate officers. As a consequence, the formal legal authority of the regulatory state has been effectively hollowed out. Fisse and Braithwaite have themselves acknowledged that, if 'the corporate form is used to obscure and deflect responsibility, whether intentionally or unintentionally, the growth of corporate activities in industrialised societies poses an acute risk of escalating breakdown of social control'.[55] Today, the regulatory state is more likely to use an axe to hack away at itself. Corporations remain free to organise themselves as private fiefdoms beyond the reach of constitutional discourse. Corporate governments do not derive their legitimacy from a solemn covenant with the people subject to their rule. Nor are they simply a useful device to promote economic growth and development.

The Power Model of the Corporation

The inherence thesis, according to which the corporation exists only because of its economic utility, is a characteristic product of American legal neoconservatism in the 1980s. Neoconservatives served as ideological shock troops in the Thatcherite and Reaganite assaults on the welfare state. If giving free rein to market forces would ensure the final triumph of democratic capitalism, it became academically plausible 'to make economics the sole determinant of the law's evolution'. Nowadays, however, according to William Bratton, 'academic corporate law leans more to power talk' than to the language of efficiency. Entity theories have challenged the economistic reduction of the corporation to a nexus of contracts. It no longer amounts to intellectual heresy to recognise 'the corporation as a complex of relationships - legal, political, and social, as well as economic'. As organisational entities, corporations combine 'hierarchical power structures' with the 'artefacts of arms-length contracting'.[56] Not for the first time, corporations are now described as 'islands of conscious power in [an] ocean of unconscious cooperation [markets] like lumps of butter coagulating in a pail of buttermilk'.[57]

Unfortunately, this new power model of the corporation replaces the simplistic doctrine that corporations owe their existence to economics with the equally misleading notion that they are inherently 'social' entities. It should be remembered that the rise of the social is an uniquely modern experience in which the public and the private realms have been collapsed into each other.[58] Politics has been transformed thereby into a perpetual conflict between more or less powerful interest groups. Within the framework of social theory, politics counts mainly as a means to an end; it has no intrinsic value as an activity through which we become most fully human. The power model of the corporation devalues politics by reducing its phenomenological significance to an uneven contest between shareholder sheep, managerial wolves and stakeholder watchdogs.[59] On this account, governmental shepherds may choose either to remain passive, acting merely as a coatrack for the contending forces, or to intervene actively as a sometimes partial referee.

The economistic view of the corporation as 'a series of bargains' is being replaced by the sociological reduction of corporate politics to 'a series of coalitions'.[60] When scholars eschew normative judgements, preferring to do no more than describe the unstable coalitions that currently control the corporate sector, they push issues of legitimate constitutional authority to one side. It is not enough to map the empirical realities of corporate power; we must also consider whether and how that power can be vested in a body of natural persons who can be held politically and legally responsible for their collective actions and omissions. The power model of the corporation displaces the responsibility that should properly be borne by managerial, professional and propertied elites onto impersonal social organisations. When corporate governance is conceived as a complex, multi-player game of the sort that once occupied deterrence theorists in the depths of the cold war, normative concerns are banished from view.

The most sustained empiricist comparison of the efficiency model with the power model is to be found in an article by Lynne Dallas. In her view, the corporation 'is an organic institution with its own internal structure and processes that impact on control of the firm'. Within that organisational structure, management is not just an 'agent'; rather, it 'holds a strategic position in the firm that it utilises to minimise the influence of other constituencies'. Similarly, Dallas accounts for shareholder voting rights, 'not on the basis of efficiency considerations', but by reference to 'a number of historical, cultural and political forces'.[61] Under the efficiency model, by contrast, shareholders enjoy their special constitutional role in corporate governance, not for any reason relevant to political theory, but because their position as residual claim holders gives them, if only through the market for corporate control, special incentives to demand efficient managerial performance.

According to Dallas, efficiency theorists misunderstand the source of shareholders' power. In her view, power within the corporation depends, in large part, upon the relative dependence of managers on resources controlled by other stakeholders. As it happens, the most important resource available to shareholders is not their capital. Modern capital markets can provide big business corporations with many alternatives to equity finance. Shareholders represent instead an ideological and political resource. In the large public corporation, 'the inclusion of shareholders in the official decision-making process' secures 'the social legitimation of managerial power'. It is because shareholders provide the ideological justification for managerial power 'that they retain their privileged role in corporate governance'. The 'formal co-optation' of shareholders into the governance structure provides managers with an 'aura of respectability'.[62] If managers are seen to be formally accountable to shareholders, managerial power is made legitimate, even though shareholders have only the most limited capacity to exercise true power in their own right. The special role of shareholders in corporate governance helps managers to justify the single-minded pursuit of profit maximisation and cost minimisation.

Under the power model, however, shareholders are just another set of stakeholders in the firm. Given the dependence of managers on resources controlled by suppliers, creditors, customers and employees, power theorists believe that the vital role of other stakeholders in the firm should be given formal recognition in its governance. Firm behaviour can best be understood, Dallas claims, not by reference to its stated objectives but by discovering 'who is in the dominant coalition'.[63] Because corporate governance rests upon a series of unstable coalitions among the various stakeholders, the firm may pursue a number of inconsistent goals simultaneously. On the basis of the power coalition model, Dallas contends that the composition and functions of boards of directors could be altered to recognise the interests of significant stakeholders without destroying the economic utility of the corporation. Such a reform strategy would further undermine the special constitutional role of shareholders. But the *membership* of other stakeholder constituencies will not assume the responsibilities of ownership. Employees, customers, suppliers and creditors will be represented by agents. Responsibility for corporate behaviour will be lodged within a vast impersonal network of agents, fiduciaries and professional negotiators who create, manage and distribute the income stream generated within the global economy. Managerial and propertied elites escape personal liability for costs and risks imposed on others by stepping behind a corporate veil. If all else fails, the burdens of personal responsibility are shifted to society at large through the device of personal liability insurance. Principals may act; agents merely conform. In particular, agents conform to impersonal behavioural norms rooted in law or convention. Principals and citizens are responsible for their actions; agents are only accountable for their behaviour.[64] As residual stakeholders, shareholders are the principals but for whom the corporate enterprise would have neither a legal personality, nor a political identity. By virtue of their residual responsibility for the firm, shareholders have a special claim to membership. But to identify shareholders as the constituent community of the corporate body politic is not to suggest that they can or should exercise power in the management of the firm. Rather, they would become a political surrogate for the elusive 'directing mind' that the law requires as the *sine qua non* of corporate criminal liability.[65] By holding active shareholders responsible for corporate misdeeds, the law could encourage them to create and sustain internal justice systems capable of preventing or punishing unlawful behaviour by agents and employees of the firm.

Corporations and the Public Policymaking Process

The power model of the corporation presents a paradox. Politics is the science of government but the power theorists have not drawn upon political theory to sharpen their insights into corporate governance. The discovery of corporate power has not given rise to a political theory of the corporation as a governmental entity, much less a civil body politic. Corporate power has been conceived as a social, rather than political or constitutional, phenomenon. Although Dallas provides an exhaustive analysis of corporate power, she never recognises in the big business corporation a private government-making public policy. She never calls the constitutional credentials of the corporation into question. Rather, she portrays corporate power as a self-enclosed, self-regulating and self-legitimating system of social control. Corporations, in this purportedly value-free perspective, may possess power and they may have policies but they are not governments. Within the orthodox academic division of labour, corporate power and corporate policies 'may be studied by economists, business administration scholars, organisational sociologists, but not normally by political scientists', [66] (nor, one might add, by constitutional jurists).

But powerful corporations do play an active and direct role in the making and enforcement of public policy. The large public corporation today has all the attributes of a 'private' government. Corporations are private, however, only in the formal sense that they are extra-constitutional entities. In law, corporations are private institutions. Their private status implies that, however powerful they might be, business corporations remain outside the formal apparatus of government. But the corporate sector has long since become a law unto itself. Once we recognise that corporations do, in fact, make and enforce public policy in their own right, the relationship between corporate power and corporate responsibility becomes a pressing constitutional problem.

Twenty years ago Mark Nadel set out a compelling case for the proposition that corporations do exercise public policymaking functions. This is so, not just because governments delegate to private organisations some of their decision-making powers (a government-sponsored job training scheme in a private industry would be one example). When governments leave a policy area unoccupied, corporations may acquire what amounts to jurisdiction in that field. Although they remain private institutions from the orthodox perspective of the constitutional lawyer or the political scientist, big business corporations have a jurisgenerative or law-making capacity of their own. They are able to shape social circumstances by allocating values (or 'goods') and risks (or 'bads') through policy outputs that are 'authoritative, binding and intentional'.[67]

Like governments, corporations allocate values by controlling the distribution of 'goods, services, honours, statuses and opportunities'. They also play a major role in the production, distribution and exchange of risks in modern society. Corporate policies can be made binding and effective through the use of sanctions. Those sanctions need not involve physical coercion or violence. It is enough if punishment takes the form of severe economic loss or a psychologically painful deprivation of social status.[68]

Corporate policies also become binding when those subject to them lose the option of resistance. This happens to the ordinary wage or salary earner when government policy dictates that taxes on income should be deducted at its source. That policy is binding because government controls the situation; it can control the conditions under which wages are paid out to employees. Corporate policies with respect to employment, investment and environmental degradation have the same sort of 'situational bindingness'.[69] Think, for example, of the public policy outputs generated by car, truck and bus manufacturers in the Western world. The automobile industry plays a very significant role in determining the ecological and personal risks that we are running in a high-intensity culture of consumption. Whenever governments choose to remain uninvolved, the automotive industry becomes a primary source of transportation, public health, land use and environmental protection policies. Decisions made by corporations in the business of producing and selling cars shape our lives. They help to create a situation we feel bound to accept.

Nadel recognises, as well, that to count as public policy, a course of corporate action or inaction must be intentional. This is particularly so when policy outputs involve the allocation of the mounting risks inherent in a society of perpetual growth. Whenever the social risks generated by corporate enterprise become known to those in charge, 'someone must decide on how much danger to allow and how to assess the costs of preventing the danger'.[70] Whenever government has failed to provide a policy of its own, it is up to corporate officials themselves to decide how much they are prepared to pay to diminish or eliminate any given risks of damage or injury to other public and private interests.

Corporate decision-makers play this public policymaking role in at least three distinct areas. All binding allocations of costs and benefits can be described as *resource transfer* policies. Taxation is a public policy output that transfers resources from one party to another. Administered pricing by oligopolistic firms is one form of corporate taxation policy. Investment policies and corporate charity also involve authoritative, binding and intentional allocations of costs and benefits. Corporations also make *regulatory* policies that involve controls over the personal conduct of employees and dealers. Manufacturers or parent corporations establish elaborate codes governing their relationship with retail distributors or franchise holders. These regulatory policies may even include a judicial system to adjudicate disputes between interested parties. When regulations allocate or transfer political power resources, corporations are setting *constituent* policies. These have to do with the structure and procedures of formal governance in a corporation or society at large. Corporate constituent policies shape not only their own internal governance structures but also the distribution of power within the internal political order of the state. Nadel identifies the old style company town as the most blatant example of the way in which corporate officials may themselves constitute and control other governmental bodies in whatever form best suits business interests. The role of corporations in campaign financing reveals the informal jurisdiction in the field of constituent policy ceded to them by governments.[71]

Power and Legitimacy in Corporate Governance

The corporate role in the public policymaking process produces outputs that are binding and intentional. But they should be regarded as authoritative only in a qualified sense. Nadel acknowledges that 'Privately made public policies may prevail even though citizens do not regard them as legitimately made'.[72] Corporations, after all, do not have a formal constitutional warrant to become public policymakers in their own right. While non-governmental public policy may be effective in practical terms, its normative justification remains uncertain and insecure.

There are those who treat de facto governmental powers wielded by corporate managers as a legitimate form of authority. But that authority provides a warrant only for the power of managers to direct the activities of their subordinates. Managerial authority arises out of the employment relationship. But it is not the promise to perform a job in return for pay that makes managerial power legitimate. A promise to work in return for pay may compel obedience as a matter of fact but it cannot provide employees with a moral justification for compliance with managerial directives of which they may disapprove. Only the essential role of managers in producing effective forms of mutually beneficial cooperation can provide employees with a principle of collective rationality, obliging them to recognise managerial authority.[73]

Stakeholders other than employees may be affected by the exercise of managerial power but they are not subject to managerial authority. According to Christopher McMahon, it is not those who are affected by managerial decision-making who must be persuaded of the legitimacy of managerial power but only 'those whose actions are guided by it'. Democratic theory does not require that everyone affected by a governmental decision should have a right to participate in it. Not everyone in the world who may be affected by American foreign policy has a right to participate in the political process leading to its formation.[74]

Managers have no power to direct the actions of customers, suppliers, creditors or citizens generally. But compliance with managerial directives can be required, morally and legally, of employees 'on the ground that cooperation to produce an outcome that each regards as morally suboptimal is often preferable to general non-cooperation either within the organisation, or with regard to a particular project'. Even employees who become victims of corporate downsizing are bound to accept the legitimacy of managerial decision-making. As a moral agent, the laid-off worker 'would find the situation in which he loses his job but the firm survives (and others keep theirs) morally preferable to the situation in which all lose their jobs'. One might suppose that the employees subject to managerial authority have a democratic right to participate in its exercise. In fact, McMahon defines democracy as 'reflexive authority, that is, the exercise of authority by those who are subject to it, and those who are subject to managerial authority are the employees'. But McMahon's theory of 'managerial democracy' is no blueprint for revolution in the corporate sector. He cheerfully concedes that, in practice, 'managerial decision-making is ultimately dictatorial'. McMahon offers 'sound moral considerations' in support of that authoritarian regime. Managers may be obliged to remain accountable to investors rather than employees by the need to achieve 'a socially optimal level of outside investment'. Even the most self-interested employee is bound to recognise the managerial prerogative to determine both the ends that direct 'mutually beneficial cooperation' and the means by which goals are to be reached. Only managers can decide when investor interests are to be given priority. Managerial expertise 'in matters of marketing, finance and engineering of all sorts' provides another ground for compliance with managerial directives.[75]

If one accepts this argument, at least some forms of corporate public policymaking can be characterised as authoritative as well as binding and intentional. But, if managerial authority is nothing more than 'a right to direct the actions of some other people',[76] other managerial powers remain without a legitimate constitutional basis. Managerial decision-making routinely allocates or withholds values affecting important stakeholder and public interests. If the corporation is conceived as a state in which only employees can become citizens,[77] relationships with outside parties become a matter of corporate foreign policy and need not be developed in a reflexive manner. But shareholders, other stakeholders and members of the public cannot be treated as aliens with no role to play in the corporate polity.

Even if all employees participated in the managerial allocation of values, the de facto power of the corporation to make public policy would not acquire moral authority in the eyes of other stakeholders or the public at large. While each employee may have individual moral concerns, it is no part of the employee's role to serve as a citizen in the corporate polity on the basis of equality. Shareholders have a better claim to become the locus of an enhanced civic authority. Ownership, especially ownership of corporate shares, cannot be reduced to 'the right to exclusive physical control of something'.[78] Even landed property in Blackstone's time had constitutional significance as the material foundation of public life and civic virtues.[79] Property *in* a corporate entity does not carry with it the right of exclusive dominion over the physical plant and equipment which remains the property *of* the corporation conceived as an entity distinct from the shareholders. Share ownership creates relations between persons who may or may not accept responsibility for the uses to which their joint property is put. In the final analysis, logic and morality tell us that both corporate property and corporate responsibility must rest with shareholders. In however vestigial a manner, the law treats shareholders not just as residual claimants to corporate property but as a body of peers bearing responsibility for corporate activities. Even limited liability implies a tiny residue of liability. But for its shareholders, the corporation would have no political, much less moral, identity. Until the best citizens among the investors become active members of the corporate body politic, neither shareholders nor managers can make public policy in an authoritative manner. At most, corporate allocations of values amount to an exercise of de facto power, based on legal control over the natural and human resources needed to organise and sustain economic life. The public policy outputs generated by corporate governments may bind those affected by them but not by virtue of a moral authority recognised by all within its reach. Corporate public policy can be made legitimate only by reconstituting the governance of the firm on republican rather than democratic capitalist or plutocratic principles. A republican model of corporate governance based upon the civic authority of shareholders would provide a constitutional challenge, not just to the de facto power of the managerial class but to the de jure authority of the state. Because any person seeking to represent particular stakeholders or public interests would be free to become an active investor in the firm, shareholders would acquire a reflexive authority of their own. Active shareholders would become the constitutional medium through which public policymaking authority migrates from the state into the reformed structures of corporate governance.

Those who adhere to the orthodox view that the right to make and enforce public policy belongs exclusively to the sovereign apparatus of state power are bound to regard the policymaking role of the corporation as illegitimate. On that positivist view of the constitution, politics and public life revolve around the struggle to control the law-making power of the state. Corporations therefore belong in the private domain of civil society where politics only rarely intrudes. Corporate law is conceived as a branch of commercial law, not of constitutional law. Nowadays, however, the political realities of corporate power are difficult to deny. It seems increasingly clear that corporations have become an integral part of the operating constitution. The question is whether the gap opening up between the dignified superstructure of governmental power and its efficient corporate base now amounts to a crisis of constitutional legitimacy.

If we abandon the positivist preoccupation with centralised sovereignty, the corporate role in public policymaking could become the subject of a new constitutional settlement. Recent work in social theory suggests that the rise of private governments is one manifestation of a global shift towards a new stage of 'reflexive' modernisation. In the first 'simple' wave of modernisation, public authority was vested exclusively in the state. This posed no major difficulties then since the corporate institutions of modern civil society were devoted, above all else, to the tasks associated with establishing mastery over nature. The first stage of modernisation now appears relatively simple because social, economic and political life revolved around the production and distribution of the wealth essential to overcome the fundamental problem of scarcity. Now the process of development itself has become problematic. Economic activity produces, not just wealth, but risks and dangers that affect all of us. As a consequence, the state is no longer the exclusive locus of the 'political'.

The Reflexive Modernisation of Corporate Power

Almost everywhere in advanced industrial societies, the 'political' has 'migrated from the official arenas - parliament, government, political administration - into the *grey zone of corporatism*'.[80] The political power to shape social circumstances has been dispersed into the corporate, scientific and professional bodies where technological innovation is conceived and executed. As a consequence, the autonomised processes of technical and economic modernisation have lost their non-political character. Given the massive proliferation of risks associated with the development of new nuclear, microelectronic and genetic technologies, corporate and scientific-technological activities have acquired a *'new political and moral dimension'*.[81]

The conventional principles and practices of responsible government have no obvious application to techno-economic processes occupying a sort of no-man's land between the political and the unpolitical. Ulrich Beck contends that the dynamic domain of corporate-technological enterprise has acquired the precarious intermediate status of a *subpolitics*, in which the scope of the social transformation set in motion by those activities are inversely proportional to their legitimacy. This implies that conventional notions of constitutional legitimacy are out of place in a society where the *'political becomes non-political and the non-political political'*.[82] As governments lapse into immobility, nongovernmental policymaking becomes increasingly important. The formal apparatus of government must then shoulder political responsibility for developments it is unable to plan or control. On the other hand, scientific, technical and economic policies loaded with political content are made routinely by corporate officials who can claim no constitutionally legitimate public authority.

According to the sociological theory of reflexive modernisation, these developments involve 'the *Freisetzung* or progressive freeing of agency from structure'.[83] In the era of simple modernity, industrial societies were dominated by the rigid structures of class, race, gender and the market. The separation of ownership and control associated with the rise of the public corporation freed managerial agents from the traditional logic of property.[84] Managerial expertise is part of the knowledge-intensive design process that replaces the material labour process in reflexive modernity. Modernity will become fully reflexive when the 'heteronomous monitoring of workers by rules is displaced by self-monitoring'. For that reason, the theory of reflexive modernisation involves 'a very "strong programme" of individualisation'.[85] Just as managerial agents were freed to reorder the structures of the market economy, workers and ordinary citizens have been freed from the innumerable constraints of class, race and gender to organise their own life narratives. The reflexive growth of the subpolitical realm can therefore be understood in the positive language of inclusion. The growth of corporate power can be viewed as the prelude to a situation where 'not only social and collective agents but individuals as well compete with the latter and each other for the emerging shaping power of the political'. Within the subpolitical realm, politicians and corporate managers must make room 'on the stage of social design' for other professional and occupational groups including the technical intelligentsia generally, as well as new social movements and other citizen initiatives.[86]

Beck's theory of reflexive modernisation is generally optimistic about the capacity of the risk society to develop new forms of self-monitoring. 'In the wake of subpoliticisation', he sees 'growing opportunities to have a voice and a share in the arrangement of society for groups hitherto uninvolved in the substantive technification and industrialisation process: citizens, the public sphere, social movements, expert groups, working people on site'. Given the courage to act, even individuals can '"move mountains" in the nerve centres of development'. Reflexive modernisation promises to enhance 'the negotiating capability of social interests'. As it does so, the 'authoritarian decision and action state gives way to the negotiation state which arranges stages and conversations and directs the show'. Under these circumstances, the 'ability of the modern state to negotiate is presumably even more important than its one-sided hierarchical ability to act, which is becoming more and more problematic'. Public life has been transformed into a vastly complex 'multilateral negotiating system, with the participation of the state'.[87]

The consequence has been to dissolve the differences between the political pursuit of power and the acquisitive drive of the entrepreneur. In the global system of needs, private wealth has been socialised through the medium of the business corporation. If *homo economicus* wants to maintain or increase his share in the wealth and income stream generated by corporate capital, he must acquire an array of sophisticated political skills. The corporation itself must become a political actor to survive and prosper in a complex regulatory environment. Observing these developments Roberto Unger, an important figure in the American critical legal studies movement, concluded that 'it's all politics'.[88] That radical slogan disguises a worrisome shift in the contemporary meaning of politics.

While the politically mediated character of the corporate system has become more obvious, the opportunities for active participation by citizens in the political processes shaping their lives is steadily shrinking. Having enlisted in the cause of reflexive modernity, Unger's response to the crisis of our times pushes corporatism to the extreme. In the radical politics of reflexive modernity everything is up for grabs. The economy is celebrated as a 'perpetual innovation machine' while the state reconstitutes itself 'as a more effective instrument for the destabilisation of entrenched plans of social division and hierarchy'.[89]

Unger rejects classical republicanism as an attempt to enshrine a canonical form of political life. The citizen, he claims, 'no longer needs to prepare the future by pretending to restore the past'.[90] Unger wants to increase opportunities for experiment and innovation in social life through the creation of a rotating capital fund that would take the place of today's private institutional and relational investors. In the ensuing micro-corporatist intermediation of interests between state agencies and a petty bourgeoisie of professionals, managers and technicians, Unger sees a vast new horizon of social plasticity and practical innovation. Absorbed within the rationalised economic machinery of experimental life, *homo politicus* trades the chance of membership in particular self-governing, civil bodies politic for a global 'citizenship of the age'[91] offered to believers in the divine economy. In Unger's empowered democracy, citizenship signifies nothing more than 'the mere circumstance of continuing involvement' in the temporary and provisional organisation of government and the economy. Accordingly, 'the importance of a clear-cut dichotomy between citizenship and residency diminishes' to the vanishing point. Like Beck, Unger recognises a subpolitical realm in which 'decisional processes within grassroots or productive organisations resemble and amplify decision-making in the central representative bodies of government'.[92] In other words, it is no longer possible to distinguish *homo economicus* from *homo politicus*.

The Risks of Refeudalisation

The theory of reflexive modernisation has direct application to the realm of corporate governance. Just as the sovereign unity of the state is subverted by the subpolitical policymaking role of the corporation, so too the presumptive identity of shareholder and corporate interests will be shattered once other stakeholders are admitted into the boardroom. If the corporation is indeed 'an island of conscious power', political realists will wonder why managers, acting on behalf of shareholders alone, should monopolise that power. Particularly as it becomes evident that employees, creditors, customers and suppliers will bear most of the risks and dangers produced by profit-hungry corporations, other voices and interests will clamour for admission to the boardroom.   The trend in corporate law towards the recognition of various stakeholder interests is another manifestation of reflexive realism in action. But for republicans, reflexive modernisation may turn out to be part of the problem and no solution at all.

Whether in the state or in the corporation, stakeholder regimes bear no resemblance to an association of persons formed with a view to some good purpose, even one so banal as profit maximisation.   Rather, corporate governance becomes another forum for negotiations within and between unstable coalitions of competing interests predisposed to mutual mistrust. Far from heralding a new era of expanded individual and corporate freedom, the theory of reflexive modernisation could signal an imminent constitutional regression in which even the gains made during the long age of the democratic revolution are threatened.   Beck himself concedes that 'the disintegration of institutions makes room for a refeudalisation of social relationships'.[93] In the politics of negotiation, all stakeholders are not created equal. Those who possess resources upon which others depend have a strong bargaining position. Those with limited bargaining power stand in need of strong protectors. Individuals who lack marketable skills or other material resources will be on their own without a protective shield. A new feudalism will emerge as dependent individuals or groups become subject to novel forms of private government combining politico-legal coercion with economic exploitation.[94]

Like the feudal polity, reflexive corporatism entails the parcellisation of sovereignty.[95] But political power in the corporate welfare state is not held by a warrior nobility, ever eager to assert its superior right to rule. In fact, contemporary elites deny the very existence of a ruling class. Power has been depersonalised, detached from kings, aristocrats and even the people, and lodged instead in corporate and professional 'expert-systems'[96] whose function it is to oversee the production of both 'goods' and 'bads' in a society of perpetual growth.   Despite their disavowal of the aristocratic principle, our corporate and professional elites have amalgamated economic exploitation with political authority, much like the feudal barons of medieval Europe. In feudal regimes 'the functions of the State were disintegrated in a vertical allocation downwards at each level of which political and economic relations were, on the other hand, integrated'.[97] Reflexive modernisation seems to be producing a corporate neo-feudalism in which political sovereignty is no longer focused in a single centre.

But the emergence of the subpolitical realm of corporate power is not the only point of contact between reflexive modernisation and the refeudalisation of civil society. Some enthusiastic sociologists hold out the hope that new sorts of paideic communities based on shared meaning and routine background practices may spring up in the gaps between the organised expert-systems dominating much of our lives. Few of these communities will resemble a traditional country village. They are more apt to be 'taste communities', rooted in the modern culture of consumption. On this analysis, individuals who transgress the distinction between the production and consumption of a particular good begin to create 'shared meanings, practices and obligations'. Fans who follow a rock group around the country or even the world, who ape its dress, and 'read and write letters to and sometimes edit the fan mags' constitute a community of taste. In the upside-down world of consumer capitalism, gay and lesbian groups count as communities but heterosexuals probably do not. Because the larger, more widely dispersed number of straights is so fractured and fragmented by competing interests and overlapping expert-systems, they are no longer bound together by shared meanings or routine background practices.[98] This sociological version of reflexive communalisation calls to mind the role of towns and cities within the feudal polity.

Feudalism provided an ideal environment for the emergence of autonomous towns. As Anderson observes, 'the feudal division of sovereignties into particularist zones with overlapping boundaries, with no universal centre of competence always permitted the existence of "allogenous" corporate entities in its interstices'.[99] The freedom of the towns was secured because local burghers were able to play feudal lords, powerful churchmen and ambitious kings against one another. No one class, estate or person achieved an absolute monopoly of law-making authority. Communal freedoms were privileges (literally, private laws) belonging to a favoured few, not civil rights open to all and sundry. The reflexive combination of communalisation and corporatism will likewise undermine the simple modern belief in a general law common to all citizens. Communities of all sorts will generate norms specific to their own particular circumstances. Affinity groups based on race, religion, gender, sexual preference or other unexpected mutations in the biopolitics of identity will press for privileges tailored to their own invented traditions.[100] Major corporations are already under pressure to expand minority hiring quotas or to extend same-sex partner benefits to their employees. Post-modern communal politics will be guided not by general rules but by the systemic need to accommodate particularistic group rights. Optimists believe that groupthink 'will often encourage an ethic of care' to counter the ruthless impersonality of the corporate system. This communitarian claim resembles the ideal of Christian charity practiced by medieval monasteries.[101] Arendt saw in charity only a worldless experience of love 'incapable of founding a public realm of its own'.[102] Nevertheless, Caesar and Mammon still come knocking on the door. If they are to provide secure havens in a heartless world, postmodern communities of taste or interest must sharpen their negotiating skills. With or without powerful protectors, all of us are forced to compete for favours in the unequal and inequitable allocation of values and risks characteristic of corporatist neo-feudalism.

Shareholders versus Stakeholders

It was in the bourgeois milieu of the medieval towns that the art of negotiation was transformed into a shared cultural practice. In an era of refeudalisation, politics becomes a highly refined, professionalised and perpetual round of negotiations between bargaining agents, each with his own as well as his principal's interests to protect. That phenomenon is visible not only in the public life of the state but also in the supposedly private realm of corporate governance. Just as the accountability gap between shareholders and managers appeared to be closing with the rise of institutional activism, other groups have challenged the norm of shareholder primacy. In the United States, several jurisdictions have enacted directors' duties laws. Under this scheme, directors may, in considering the best interests of the corporation, weigh the effects of any action, not just on shareholders, but on employees, suppliers, creditors and other stakeholders in the enterprise as a whole. Those who favour this and similar reforms 'emphasise that management's responsibility to look after non-shareholders arises in the context of a more general duty to further the success of the corporation as a whole, conceived as a complex network of shareholders and non-shareholders'.[103]

David Millon frankly acknowledges that stakeholder laws of this sort establish an 'oligarchy' in which corporate management exercises a political discretion over resource allocation and the distribution of corporate wealth. Not only will these political issues of wealth distribution 'be committed to the discretion of private individuals'; the meaning of both 'ownership' and 'membership' in the corporation will be radically altered. Some see in stakeholder laws 'manifestations of a deeper design to enhance the status of non-shareholders within the corporate enterprise'. This would require a reallocation of power resources so as to promote greater non-shareholder involvement in the decision-making process. At a minimum, this will require formal negotiations between managers and stakeholders. It could extend to granting stakeholders a share in corporate control, either through representation on boards of directors or through voting rights. Especially since stakeholders need not have any permanent relationship with the firm, these developments would debase and devalue the meaning of membership in the body corporate. But 'if nonshareholders are to have powers of control, perhaps new ownership structures should be considered as well'.[104] Within the novel ownership and membership structure of the reflexive corporation, stakeholders will not encounter one another as political equals. Rather the political realities of power will sort them into a hierarchy of functional relevance to important corporate goals and interests. This neo-feudal strategy will entrench a managerial oligarchy empowered to mediate between competing stakeholders like a feudal baron holding court before his squabbling vassals. This is hardly an appealing prospect. Nor is the programmatic alternative most often touted in the academic literature or corporate governance. According to the experts in this field, reformers must choose between the neo-feudal stakeholder strategy and the reconstitution of finance capital as a surrogate for society as a whole.

Both refeudalisation and the restored reign of finance capital privilege the role of the bourgeois in corporate governance over that of the citizen. The stakeholder model acknowledges the political and public dimension of corporate governance but rejects the primacy of the shareholder within the corporate constitution. Institutional activism, on the other hand, restores the primacy of the shareholder while reducing the corporation to a mere investment vehicle devoid of political or constitutional significance. We need to reconstitute the corporation as an investment vehicle wherein the best citizens among the shareholders agree to accept responsibility for the political direction of the corporate enterprise, while leaving to managers and other stakeholders the efficient and effective performance of their own specialised economic functions. In the republican model of corporate governance, both ownership and membership in the joint enterprise would acquire a new measure of constitutional significance. Ownership of corporate property beyond a prescribed minimum would entitle one to participate as an equal in the governance of the enterprise as a whole.

By distinguishing between active and passive investors while insisting that active investors encounter each other as citizens and not simply as bourgeois, the corporate constitution can be adapted to both the economic logic of efficiency and the political realities of power. By reconstituting the corporation as a civil body politic, managerial, professional and propertied elites could recover the constitutional authority they steadfastly renounced during the era of simple modernisation. Then, the bourgeois ruled the corporate sector while the democratic citizen became the touchstone of legitimacy for the rising nation-state. In a world of multiplying, often invisible risks generated by the absolute imperative of capitalist development, we need a natural aristocracy of property owners capable of assuming personal, as well as political, responsibility for the use and misuse of their corporate power. In principle, every joint enterprise could provide a vehicle for this sort of civic elite. But the republican model of the corporation as a civil body politic has its most obvious application to corporations that perform important public services.

But, even if we have established the political need for a republican model of corporate governance, it remains to be seen whether such a reform strategy remains possible. One could concede the limitations of both institutional shareholder activism and the efficiency model of the corporation that provides its theoretical justification, just as one could remain disturbed by the normative blind spot built into the power coalition model, while seeing in the republican solution little more than another utopian fantasy. Is it really possible that the shareholder, the most fickle and self-interested specimen of *homo economicus*, might someday metamorphose into a public-spirited aristocrat?

Notes

1   Ronald J Gilson, 'Evaluating Dual Class Common Stock: The Relevance of Substitutes' (1987) 73 *Virginia Law Review* 807 at pp 824-32.
2   R Eells, *The Government of Corporations* (New York: Free Press, 1962).
3   Mark J Roe, *Strong Managers, Weak Owners: The Political Roots of American Corporate Finance* (Princeton: Princeton University Press, 1994).
4   Michael C Jensen, 'Eclipse of the Public Corporation' *Harvard Business Review* (September-October 1989).
5   Gilson, *supra* note 1 at p 809.
6   *Ibid*, p 810.
7   Jensen, *supra* note 4 at p 65.
8   *Ibid*, pp 65-6.
9   *Ibid*, p 61.
10   *Ibid*, p 64.
11   *Ibid*, pp 66, 70.
12   *Ibid*, p 67.
13   *Ibid*, p 67.
14   Jay O Light, 'The Privatization of Equity' *Harvard Business Review* (September-October 1989) pp 42-3.
15   Cf Ron Chernow, *The House of Morgan: An American Banking Dynasty and the Rise of Modern Finance* (New York: Simon and Schuster 1990).

16   Robert A G Monks and Nell Minow, *Power and Accountability* (New York: Harper, 1991) p 240.
17   *Ibid*, pp 243, 262.
18   John C Coffee, Jr, 'Liquidity versus Control: The Institutional Investor as Corporate Monitor' (1991) 91 *Columbia Law Review* 1277 at p 1352.
19   Cf Frederick Lewis Allen, *The Lords of Creation* (New York: Harper, 1935).
20   Bernard S Black, 'Shareholder Passivity Re-examined' (1990) 89 *Michigan Law Review* 520 at 523.
21   *Ibid*, p 525.
22   Edward B Rock, 'The Logic and (Uncertain) Significance of Institutional Shareholder Activism' (1991) 79 *Georgetown Law Journal* 445.
23   *Ibid*, pp 473, 469, 451, 486.
24   Monks and Minow, *supra* note 16 at p 240.
25   Roe, *supra* note 3 at p 237.
26   Monks and Minow, *supra* note 16 at pp 65-6.
27   Roe, *supra* note 3 at pp viii-ix.
28   Walter Werner, 'Corporation Law in Search of its Future' (1981) 81 *Columbia Law Review* 1611.
29   James Willard Hurst, *The Legitimacy of the Business Corporation in the Law of the United States 1780-1970* (Charlottesville: University Press of Virginia, 1970) pp 26, 28.
30   Roe, *supra* note 3 at pp vii, xiv.
31   *Ibid*, pp 29, 42-5.
32   *Ibid*, pp 233-4, 285-6.
33   *Ibid*, pp 285-6.
34   Edward Rock, 'Controlling the Dark Side of Relational Investing' (1994) 15 *Cardozo Law Review* 987.
35   Rock, *supra* note 22 at p 506.
36   Rock, *supra* note 34, at p 988.
37   Rock, *supra* note 22 at p 506.
38   Rock, *supra* note 34 at pp 989, 1003.
39   *Ibid*, 1003, 1030, 1021-2.
40   Cf Richard Hofstadter, *The Paranoid Style in American Politics and Other Essays* (New York: Knopf, 1965); Lawrence Goodwyn, *Democratic Promise: The Populist Movement in America* (New York: Oxford University Press, 1976); Andrew Fraser, 'Populism and Republican Jurisprudence' *Telos* 88 (Summer 1991) pp 95-110.
41   Marvin Meyers, *The Jacksonian Persuasion: Politics and Belief* (New York: Vintage, 1960); Richard Hofstadter, *The Age of Reform: From Bryan to FDR* (New York: Vintage, 1955).
42   Late nineteenth century American populism had nothing to say on the problem of corporate governance. Cf Goodwyn *supra* note 40. On the managerial revolution, see Samuel Francis, *Beautiful Losers: Essays on the Failure of American Conservatism* (Columbia: University of Missouri Press, 1993); Paul Gottfried 'Public Administration and Liberal Democracy' *Telos* 104 (Summer 1995) pp 27-50; and James Burnham, *The Managerial Revolution* (London: Putnam, 1942).
43   Roe, *supra* note 3 at p 283.

44   Rock, *supra* note 34 at p 1031.
45   Roe, *supra* note 3 at p 24.
46   Monks and Minow, *supra* note 16 at pp 239-66.
47   Benjamin Barber, *Strong Democracy: Participatory Politics for a New Age* (Berkeley: University of California Press, 1984) p 220.
48   Milton Friedman, *Capitalism and Freedom* (Chicago: University of Chicago Press, 1982) p 133.
49   Barber, *supra* note 47 at p 219.
50   Cf R Jeffrey Lustig, *Corporate Liberalism: The Origins of Modern American Political Theory, 1890-1920* (Berkeley: University of California Press, 1982) p 113.
51   Jeffrey N Gordon, 'Shareholder Initiative: A Social Choice and Game Theoretic Approach to Corporate Law' (1991) 60 *Cincinnati Law Review* 347 at pp 353, 361.
52   Brent Fisse and John Braithwaite, *Corporations, Crime and Accountability* (Cambridge: Cambridge University Press, 1993) pp 12, 14-15.
53   Ambrose Bierce, *The Devil's Dictionary*, quoted in *ibid* p 15.
54   *Ibid*, p 15.
55   *Ibid*, p 14.
56   William W Bratton, 'The Economic Structure of the Post-Contractual Corporation' (1992) 87 *Northwestern University Law Review* 180 at pp 197, 185, 212.
57   Dennis Robertson, quoted in Richard P Adelstein, 'Islands of Conscious Power: Louis D Brandeis and the Modern Corporation' (1989) 63 *Business History Review* 614 at p 636.
58   Hannah Arendt, *The Human Condition* (Chicago: University of Chicago Press, 1958).
59   Cf Lynne L Dallas, 'Two Models of Corporate Governance: Beyond Berle and Means' (1988) 22 *University of Michigan Journal of Law Reform* 19.
60   Frank H Easterbrook and Daniel R Fischel, *The Economic Structure of Corporate Law* (Cambridge, MA: Harvard University Press, 1991); John C Coffee, Jr, 'Unstable Coalitions: Corporate Governance as a Multi-Player Game' (1990) 78 *Georgetown Law Journal* 1495.
61   Dallas, *supra* note 59 at pp 25-6.
62   *Ibid*, pp 65, 72, 94-6.
63   *Ibid*, p 31.
64   Arendt, *supra* note 58 at pp 41-5.
65   *Tesco Supermarkets Ltd v Nattras* [1972] AC 153.
66   Mark Nadel, 'The Hidden Dimensions of Public Policy: Private Governments and the Policy-making Process' (1975) 37 *Journal of Politics* 2 at p 5.
67   *Ibid*, pp 14-15.
68   *Ibid*, pp 15-19.
69   *Ibid*, p 18.
70   *Ibid*, p 20.
71   *Ibid*, pp 21-31.
72   *Ibid*, p 19.
73   Christopher McMahon, *Authority and Democracy: A General Theory of Government and Management* (Princeton: Princeton University Press, 1994) pp 27, 6-7, 102-8.
74   *Ibid*, pp 10-12.
75   *Ibid*, pp 249, 255-6, 13, 258-9, 269, 272.

76   *Ibid*, p 27.

77   *Ibid*, p 10.

78   *Ibid*, p 16.

79   J G A Pocock, ed, *The Political Works of James Harrington* (Cambridge: Cambridge University Press, 1977); William Blackstone, *Commentaries on the Laws of England* Vol I (Chicago: University of Chicago Press, 1979) p 165.

80   Ulrich Beck, *Risk Society: Towards a New Modernity*, tr Mark Ritter (London: Sage, 1992) p 188 [emphasis in original].

81   *Ibid*, p 186 [emphasis in original].

82   *Ibid*, p 186 [emphasis in original].

83   Scott Lash, 'Reflexivity and its Doubles: Structure, Aesthetics, Community' in Ulrich Beck, *et al, Reflexive Modernization: Politics, Tradition and Aesthetics in the Modern Social Order* (Oxford: Polity, 1994) p 119.

84   Adolf A Berle, Jr and Gardiner C Means, *The Modern Corporation and Private Property* (New York: Macmillan, 1933) pp 333-9.

85   Lash, *supra* note 83 at pp 119, 111.

86   Ulrich Beck, 'The Reinvention of Politics: Towards a Theory of Reflexive Modernization' in Ulrich Beck, *et al, supra* note 83 at p 22.

87   *Ibid*, pp 23, 34-40.

88   Roberto Mangabeira Unger, *Social Theory: Its Situation and Its Task*, Vol 1 of *Politics : A Work in Constructive Social Theory* (Cambridge: Cambridge University Press, 1987) pp 151-169; see also, Andrew Fraser, 'Reconstituting Enlightened Despotism' *Telos* 78 (Winter 1988-89) pp 169-182.

89   Roberto Mangabeira Unger, *False Necessity: Social Theory in the Service of Radical Democracy* Vol 2, of *Politics: A Work in Constructive Social Theory* (Cambridge: Cambridge University Press, 1987) pp 491, 551.

90   *Ibid*, p 588.

91   Unger, *Social Theory, supra* note 88 at p 113.

92   Unger, *False Necessity, supra* note 89 at pp 529-530.

93   *Ibid*, p 44. See also Ingeborg Maus, 'Sinn and Bedeutung von Volkssouveranität in der modernern Gesellschaft' (1991) 24 *Kritische Justiz* 137 at p 141.

94   Cf Perry Anderson, *Passages from Antiquity to Feudalism* (London: New Left Books, 1974) p 147.

95   *Ibid*, p 150.

96   Cf Anthony Giddens, 'Living in a Post-Traditional Society' in Ulrich Beck *et al, supra* note 83.

97   Anderson, *supra* note 94 at p 148.

98   Lash, *supra* note 83 at pp 157-69.

99   Anderson, *supra* note 94 at p 148.

100   John Fekete, *Moral Panic: Biopolitics Rising* (Montreal: Robert Davies, 1994); Rainer Knopff (with Thomas Flanagan) *Human Rights and Social Technology: The New War on Discrimination* (Ottawa: Carleton University Press, 1989).

101   Lash, *supra* note 83 at pp 157, 164.

102   Arendt, *supra* note 58 at p 53.

103   David Millon, 'Redefining Corporate Law' (1991) 24 *Indiana Law Review* 223 at p 270.

104   *Ibid*, pp 274-7.

4 Corporations and the Constitutional Genesis of Civic Authority

Introduction

To propose that a class of bourgeois shareholders be transformed into a senatorial elite is to risk one's political credibility. But to reject such a proposal out of hand is to expose one's confinement within the narrow ideological boundaries of contemporary constitutional and legal discourse. Certainly a review of the extensive academic literature on corporate governance reveals no movement to challenge the established regime of corporate power. That body of scholarship does provide a wealth of expert testimony to the effect that there is no imaginable alternative to the forms of corporate governance that have been developed in the major bourgeois liberal republics of the late twentieth century. Throughout the Anglo-American civilisation that includes Australia and New Zealand, as well as Canada, the conventional limits of constitutional reform within the corporate sector are defined by the international best practice standard laid down by the Germans and the Japanese. In our spectacular society of perpetual growth,[1] the archaic ideals of classical political theory seem out of touch with reality. The past is dead and lies buried beneath the sprawling expanse of corporate theme parks, while the future has been programmed as a continuation of present trends.

The consequent failure of political imagination reflects not just the material power of the corporate sector but also the ideological hegemony of a certain concept of the corporation. To conceive of the corporation solely in the instrumental, utilitarian language of economics is to deny the relevance of political theory to the empirical and normative analysis of corporate governance. Not even the organisational sociologists studying the role of power relations in corporate enterprise can do anything more than map the social realities of power without a theory explaining how, why and whether corporations should act as private governments. Political theory can help us

91

to understand the realities of corporate power; it can also suggest strategies to make the exercise of that power constitutionally legitimate. If constitutional and legal discourse can be influenced by a political model of the corporation, new avenues of reform may begin to suggest themselves to our collective political imagination.

Until recently, the clash between the inherence thesis and the erosion thesis defined the terms and limits of the debate over corporate governance. One side deplores the erosion of shareholder democracy. The other stock response dismisses the myth of the active shareholder as irrelevant to the actual history of the big business corporation. Both sides agree that corporations serve a vital economic function by providing firm central direction to the enterprising use of pooled assets. Whatever their attitudes to the governance of corporations, experts of all stripes revere the corporate capacity to produce wealth. There has been less public or academic attention paid to the role of corporations in the generation of political power. We need a republican model of the corporation as a civil body politic to call the constitutional credentials of *freigesetzte*, autolegitimating corporate power into question.

Throughout the first, simple phase of capitalist modernisation, corporate power was justified in measures of economic performance. Not surprisingly, the central political drama of classical industrial society brought capital and labour into conflict over the role of the state in the distribution of the wealth amassed through capitalist development and imperial expansion. The onset of a second, reflexive stage of modernisation is marked by the emergence of new sources of conflict and the decay of older 'formations of class, stratum, occupation, sex roles, nuclear family, plant, business sectors, and of course also the prerequisites and continuing forms of natural techno-economic progress'. Class warfare seems to be a thing of the past. The conflicts characteristic of an emergent reflexive modernity focus on the multiplying risks and insecurities created by a global society of perpetual growth. The risks of nuclear catastrophe, environmental disaster and economic obsolescence are not confined to members of any one class, race or gender. According to Ulrich Beck, 'the distributional conflicts over "goods" (income, jobs, social security)' that rocked the foundations of simple industrial societies have been 'covered over by the distributional conflicts over "bads"'.[2] These clashes revolve around the distribution of responsibility, not of wealth. In these altered circumstances, the power of the corporation should depend upon its political legitimacy and not just its economic utility.

The basic framework of corporate governance in the bourgeois liberal republics, whatever the difference between German, Japanese and Anglo-

American models, is the product of a simpler stage of development. Corporate success is no longer simply a matter of maintaining a healthy bottom line. Forms of corporate governance designed to facilitate the production of wealth and power must now be adapted to cope with conflicts erupting over the corporate production of risks. Corporate governments in the age of reflexive modernity already formulate policies affecting a wide range of public and private interests. Corporations must establish policy production rules determining 'how the risks accompanying goods production (nuclear and chemical mega-technology, genetic research, the threat to the environment, overmilitarisation and the increasing emiseration outside of western industrial society) can be distributed, prevented, controlled and legitimised'.[3] If we return to the first principles of classical political theory, we can revive the embryonic republican model of the corporation as a civil body politic. Moved by the spirit of a republican reformation, that concept could evolve into an institutional form better adapted to the challenges of reflexive modernisation than the soulless, and quite possibly obsolescent, public corporation.

The Evolutionary Thesis

If the sociologists of reflexive modernisation can be believed, forms of corporate governance designed to maximise the production of wealth, while minimising the responsibilities of the wealthy, will be subject to increasing conflict. Constitutional change of some sort is probably inevitable. If that transformation is to preserve the positive political and constitutional gains associated with the age of the democratic revolution, the modern business corporation must be constitutionalised. As things stand, the de facto powers of governance vested in big business are steadily hollowing out the constitutional edifice of the bourgeois liberal republic. At the moment of modern capitalism's final victory over both communism and fascism, we face the 'coming tyranny' of 'an economic regime of unaccountable rulers, a totalitarianism not of the political sphere but of the economic'.[4] The idea of the corporation as a little republic must become something more than a mere metaphor. Neither the efficiency model nor the power model of the corporation is adequate to the requirements of reflexive modernisation. The one denies that rational economic actors could ever, or did ever, choose to constitute the business corporation as a civil body politic. The other holds fast to a simple-minded realism. On this view, shareholder democracy is no more than a lost corporate Eden, beyond hope of recovery. The republican reformation of corporate governance will reject both the erosion doctrine of original sin and the inherence theory of predestination. Political theory and constitutional jurisprudence alike will draw upon an evolutionary theory of the corporation as an organisational form capable of constitutional development through creative adaptation to altered circumstances. The demands of wealth production favoured the separation of ownership and control in the simple phase of capitalist modernisation. In a reflexive corporate polity sensitive to the production and management of risk, managerial power will be separated from the authority wielded by shareholders. With authority comes responsibility. The converse also holds true. By assuming the political burden of corporate social responsibility, active shareholders would don the mantle of legitimate constitutional authority.

Erosion theorists claim that the republican model of the corporation was tried and found wanting in the early stages of capitalist development.[5] Most have concluded that there is no point in flogging a dead horse. One could just as easily suggest that the Anglo-American concept of the civil body politic was ahead of its time in a society where the political utility of the corporation was quickly subordinated to its economic role as a legal technology vital to the efficient production of wealth. On this view, the early American business corporation could be constituted as a civil body politic only in the most embryonic of forms.[6] As with the Mayflower Compact, their appearance in American society reflected 'the elementary structure of joint enterprise'.[7] In the days when corporate charters routinely constituted the enterprise as a body politic, there was no possibility of separating the political utility of the corporate enterprise from its economic goals.

Prior to the American Revolution, the corporate body politic was not automatically subordinated to the lordship of capital. A complex fusion of political and economic concerns was reflected in the pre-modern, traditional elements in the constitution of ventures such as the East India Company, the Hudson's Bay Company or even the Massachusetts Bay Company. Those enterprises owed their existence to a complex amalgam of royal, aristocratic and bourgeois interests. Widely divergent interests were bound together in a legal form that readily called to mind the image of a little republic. The charters themselves were the instruments of a royal power that had its own fish to fry. The bourgeois ambitions and interests served by the East India Company were plain to see.[8] But it was also true that the role of the bourgeois shareholder could be played just as easily by a royal courtier, or the king himself as by an urban merchant with aspirations towards a landed estate, perhaps even an aristocratic title. The bourgeois stake in the enterprise was reflected in the fact that votes were attached to shares, not shareholders. But, even though each share carried one vote, their par value was set at £500. With the price of a single share set at such a high level, there must have been a rough parity among a relatively limited number of large investors. No doubt the high par value also served to reassure patrician shareholders that they were indeed members of an honourable company of adventurers and not a déclassé collection of money-grubbing merchants and tradesmen. The early modern chartered trading company brought patrician landowners and aristocratic insiders together with bourgeois interests in joint enterprises serving the political as well as the economic needs of the shareholders.

Once the democratic revolution destroyed the power of kings and aristocracies, while progressively undermining the formal constitutional significance of property ownership, the corporation as a civil body politic lost its raison d'être. For a time, conservative lawyers in the early American republic struggled to preserve the capacity of the corporation to straddle the boundary between the private and the public domains. In the end, their efforts were in vain. As legal discourse succumbed to the simple-minded logic of capital accumulation, corporate lawyers rejected the notion of the civil body politic as an outdated anachronism.

In the evolutionary process, an idea, norm or institution out of step with the legal *Zeitgeist* at one stage of historical development may flower into unexpected relevance when faced with the novel challenges of another era. Development is evolutionary in that the civil body politic could be foreshadowed, but not fully realised, prior to the era of reflexive modernisation. Only now can the republican model of the corporation give fresh meaning to an ideal of civic freedom rooted in the Greek discovery of politics.[9]

No more than the germ of a possibility in the age of the democratic revolution, the corporate republic may be the sort of evolutionary adaptation essential to constitutional survival in a more complex and riskier environment. In biological evolution, mere survival does not 'imply superiority to untried alternatives'.[10] A destroyed group in *yesterday's* environment might have turned out to be a survivor in *today's* environment. But, having been naturally selected for extinction in the struggle to survive, yesterday's losers will never get the chance to become today's evolutionary winners. In the process of constitutional evolution, by contrast, we have the historical memory of countless untried and failed alternatives still available to us. As humans we also possess the power of reasoned speech. Through the exercise of that faculty we can try to define the nature of the good life and how it might be realised in the circumstances of our own time. It should be through a process of rational rather than natural selection that citizens choose between paths of development. In principle, we are not completely dependent upon paths already taken. Untried and failed alternatives from the past can be resurrected in an altered environment.

Another influential interpretation of the legal history of the corporation stresses the element of historical continuity while obscuring both the need for and the possibility of evolutionary development. The contemporary problems of corporate law simply replicate the conflicts of the past. On this view, lawyers have always been faced with the recurrent choice between two competing concepts of the corporation: the organic and the artificial. No other alternative seems to be available. The legal history of the corporation reveals only a timeless struggle for ascendancy between the fellowship principle and the lordship principle. Faced with the artificial and mechanical world of corporate capitalism, it is all too natural to long for the organic harmony of a vanished corporate fellowship. In one last moment of romantic resistance to the simple logic of capitalist modernisation, many prominent Anglo-American legal scholars around the turn of the twentieth century were influenced by the sweeping historical vision of Otto von Gierke.[11] In place of the arid doctrine that the corporation was a mere legal fiction, Gierke offered the vision of the corporation as an organic entity with a life and personality of its own. For Gierke, the medieval guild was but one of many early forms of Germanic fellowship whose organic nature was denied by the imperial logic of Roman law. The fiction theory of the corporation was a product of the medieval papacy. According to this Romanist doctrine, the corporation is an artificial creature of the sovereign will, possessing only those powers and capacities spelled out in its charter. A descending theory of authority based on the Roman *imperium* was set in dramatic and eternal opposition to the Germanic *Volksgeist*.[12]

In the modern era, Gierke saw the medieval struggle between fellowship and lordship being played out again in the development of novel forms of association ranging from producers cooperatives to joint-stock companies. For Gierke, the cooperative was the purest modern expression of the fellowship principle. In his early days, when he was suspected by some of republican leanings, Gierke could not have escaped gloom as he pondered the future of cooperative associations in the civil society largely organised and managed by the modern business corporation (*Aktiengesellschaft*). While he acknowledged that the joint-stock company was beneficial and necessary 'as a link in the chain of economic organisms', he feared that 'if it alone ruled it would lead to the despotism of capital'.[13]

By portraying corporate legal history as an eternal conflict between fellowship and lordship, Gierke and his Anglo-American disciples missed the evolutionary potential of the corporate form. While the Gierkean progressives sought to defend the associational element of corporate life against the domination of capital, the Germanic obsession with the problem of corporate personality led to an intellectual and political dead end. The only alternative to the despotic reign of corporate capital was a recycled version of the medieval guild. By stressing the organic unity of the corporate fellowship, Gierke could not anticipate the modern stakeholder polity embracing a plurality of competing and contradictory interests, all clamouring for recognition. Nor did he defend the special civic role of shareholders against the political push by stakeholders to be recognised as constituent elements in a neo-feudal corporate polity. Gierke did, of course, recognise that medieval fellowships differed from the modern business firm. In the medieval guild, fellowship embraced the whole life of the member. Nowadays, 'freely formed' associations are confined to a single specified purpose. While the medieval corporation fettered 'the individual, the modern association is compatible with the greatest conceivable personal freedom'. Members of modern associations 'unite only so far as is requisite for one quite specific purpose'. The 'old system of corporations united the *fellows* as closely as possible, in order to distinguish the fellow*ships* all the more clearly from one another'. Today, paper fellowships have become indistinguishable from each other in the corporate pursuit of wealth and power while fictive fellows turn into self-interested surrogates for share certificates scattered across the face of the globe. In the divine economy, 'one collective unity' is constructed out of corporate entities 'interlocking with one another in a hundred different ways'.[14] But neither the medieval guild nor the modern corporation form an assembly of political peers sharing in authority. Fellowship is not synonymous with citizenship. Nor can the liquid capital of the individual shareholder be locked into the organic unity of a corporate fellowship. Gierke recognised that the fellowship of shareholders in the modern business corporation was dangerously attenuated. He never imagined that bourgeois investors could reinvent citizenship in a distinctively modern corporate polity.

The structure of medieval 'communal life was modelled on the relationships between the members of a family because they were known to be non-political and even anti-political'.[15] For Gierke, 'the organism of the joint stock company is no different from other organisms based on fellowship', each with its own 'personal *collective will*'.[16] In our time, the impersonal power of social capital has taken on a life of its own. In the end, the vestigial traces of the fellowship principle in the constitution of the corporation offered little resistance to the lordship of capital. The modern business firm is an 'organisation of capital' not an 'organisation of people'.[17] As such, it exists to produce wealth for its shareholders and to minimise their responsibility for the social and ecological costs of corporate behaviour. Gierkeans got to the point of recognising that the railways were as real as Lancashire, but often forgot that social capital was the ghost driving the machine.[18] They asked only that corporations be held legally liable for tortious and criminal behaviour.[19] Their reformist vision reached its apogee in a plodding programme of guild socialism in which the railways would be governed by and for the workers in that industry just as if the communalism of medieval Lancashire had been restored in the modern county council. Guild socialism was based upon a model of functional feudalism that presupposed a mutuality of interest between employees and other stakeholders in the corporate enterprise.[20] The corporation conceived in feudal and familial terms of fraternity cannot be squared with the civic model of the corporation as an association of free, equal and independent personalities. Nor can the static ideal of corporate fellowship help us to confront the challenges of reflexive modernisation. The business corporation will become a civil body politic, not because it has always possessed an organic legal personality, but because modern legal artifice could reconstitute a powerful instrument of wealth creation into a legitimate political entity.

Reflexivity has been defined as 'self-confrontation with the effects of risk society'.[21] That will become possible only when public spheres are constituted in the corporate sector. A plurality of interests and values must find a voice on the basis of equality within the corporate policymaking process. So far, fellowship has not counted for much in the history of the modern business corporation. The only other alternative to the lordship of capital is the citizenship principle. It may be that the civil body politic had only a limited role to play in the middle ages or in the era of simple modernisation. But the onset of reflexive modernity marks the moment of its evolutionary appearance as a necessary constitutional adaptation if the telos of republican freedom is to preserve its place in a common civic culture. Mature forms of the civil body politic may now develop beyond the elementary structure of joint enterprise recognised in the corporate law of the early modern era. A simple fellowship model of shareholder democracy was of dubious worth in the early American republic. It has almost no relevance today.

The Separation of Power and Authority

Contemporary Australia provides many examples of shareholder democracies that have succumbed to the evolutionary shocks of deregulated global capitalism. Various building societies and the National Roads and Motorists Association (NRMA) have been prime candidates for corporate takeovers or floats in the recent past. During the metamorphosis of such mutual or cooperative societies into publicly listed corporations, the fellowship principle has been quietly displaced by the lordship of capital. Whatever the size of one's account, every building society customer became a member and received a single vote at general meetings and in postal ballots. Similarly, the purchaser of emergency roadside services from the NRMA becomes a member of the association with full voting rights on the basis of one person, one vote. As small, mutual aid societies, these associations may once have resembled a Gierkean corporate fellowship. Once they grew into large and successful commercial enterprises, most of the ostensible owners of the cooperative societies retained little interest in corporate control. Members would often be only dimly aware of their constitutional role within the organisation, with relatively few bothering to exercise their voting rights. As a consequence, these institutions were bound to fall under the effective control of managerial or stakeholder oligarchies of some sort. With the moves towards deregulation of the financial services industry, pressures grew to exploit the assets and opportunities belonging to the mutual aid societies more effectively by transforming them into corporations providing banking and other financial services.

To encourage approval for the corporate takeovers and public floats, members have been offered payments in cash or shares in return for the surrender of their existing membership and voting rights. For the vast majority of passive members who had scant interest in the political rights and privileges attached to their investment, these offers are typically too good to resist. The building societies and the NRMA are fellowships in form only, not in substance. Many members, each with a comparatively small stake in the enterprise: such institutional properties pose formidable collective action problems even when investors have equal voting rights. The paradox here is that the property element in membership of mutual aid societies could be weighted more heavily in such a way as to enhance its associational significance. In other words, the mutual societies could have adopted a dual class capital structure, transforming the corporate polity from a shareholder democracy masking an insider oligarchy into an aristocratic republic giving real constitutional meaning to the oxymoronic ideal of democratic capitalism.

To accomplish that change, most members of commercialised mutual aid societies could have become shareholders in a new corporate entity but would not have retained voting rights. They would simply continue on as passive investors, receiving some form of compensation for the surrender of their political rights.   Only those investors who acquired a significant threshold equity stake in the enterprise would be entitled to vote. But the corporate franchise would be exercised on the basis of one voice, one vote. Such a corporate structure might not always be appropriate to the circumstances of particular firms in particular industries. Judgements on that issue will depend upon the relative importance of political reflexivity to the governance of any given enterprise, industry or occupation.

In principle, every corporation or professional association actively engaged in the production, distribution and exchange of 'bads' stands in need of governance structures that can distribute responsibility in a fair and effective manner. But the main thrust of modern corporate law has been to absolve shareholders of responsibility for corporate deeds and misdeeds alike. By creating a political class of active investors who can provide an enterprise, not just with capital, but with critical intelligence and professional commitment as well, business corporations could adapt to the constitutional and ethical imperatives of reflexive modernisation.   Every active investor would be incorporated into an association of political peers responsible for the direction of the joint venture. In exercising his political rights, the active investor would assume responsibility for the 'negative externalities' that, but for the corporation, would not have come into being. Among the risks that must be managed by any governing body of active investors is the danger of business failure. That risk is certain to be magnified if shortsighted and ill-informed shareholders regularly second-guess managerial decisions concerning the production and distribution of goods. On the other hand, managers who reject 'irresponsible talk of risk' as a threat to economic recovery and job creation may be equally myopic. Large corporations and their managements may later have to pay a heavy economic price for evading risks today. As Ulrich Beck cautions:

> Neurotechnology and human genetic engineering violate deep-seated cultural taboos. At the same time, they require billions in investment. Those who would hush up or sweep aside the uneasiness of the general public are building research empires and markets on quicksand. If risk society becomes sceptical towards technology, such investments can be suicidal. The nuclear energy industry could tell us a thing or two about that.[22]

By fattening cattle on the diseased remains of dead sheep, British feed lot operators violated a popular taboo against turning herbivores into carnivores. The Mad Cow Disease scare that followed gives the corporate chieftains of the British beef industry a story of their own to tell.

In the risk society, economic success and a reflexive corporate polity must become interdependent elements of a virtuous circle. But this does not mean that active investors should usurp managerial functions. The role of the active shareholder in a republican governance structure is not to rob managers of their power to run a business effectively. Rather, it is to provide an independent locus of authority in the corporate constitution. Within the reflexive corporation, the active shareholders would play the role once reserved for the Roman Senate. In the Roman constitution, power was said to reside in the people, while 'authority rests with the Senate'.[23] The role of the Senate was to augment the power of the people. Active investors will augment managerial power, not just by monitoring the bottom line indices of performance, but by accepting public responsibility for the negative externalities arising as a consequence of corrupt, careless or callous corporate conduct.

Shareholders would not become the new masters of the corporation, issuing orders to their managerial hirelings. As Arendt remarks, 'the most conspicuous characteristic of those in authority is that they do not have power'. Like the authority of the Roman Senate, the augmentation that the active shareholders must add to managerial decisions is not power. For that reason 'it seems to us curiously elusive and intangible, bearing in this respect a striking resemblance to Montesquieu's judiciary branch of government, whose power he called "somehow nil" (*en quelque façon nulle*) and which nevertheless constitutes the highest authority in constitutional governments'.[24]

The actual appearance of such corporate senates must occur as part of a more general movement aimed at the republican reformation of the corporate welfare state. Transforming active investors into corporate senators would be linked to other changes in the received doctrines of corporate law. Whether active investors could be genuinely responsible for their corporate conduct if they retain the privilege of limited liability is one question that would flow from the creation of a shareholder senate. Limited liability may continue to make sense in respect of common shareholders who hold no political rights in the corporate body. But if some shareholders choose to select themselves as members of a corporate senate authorised to oversee and discipline the exercise of managerial power, there is no obvious reason to shield them from tortious or criminal liability for the natural and ordinary consequences of their actions. Nor is it obvious that *unlimited* personal liability is the best or only way to make shareholders exercise their authority in a responsible and effective manner. Whatever the details of a reformed corporations law, it will require legislative action and judicial sanction to become the foundation of a new constitutional settlement within modern civil society. Without widespread popular and professional support, any such legal changes will never manage to transform the political culture of corporate governance.

In the absence of a political, social and even spiritual movement towards the republican reformation of Anglo-American civilisation, we face the prospect of refeudalisation. By reconstituting the governance of the corporate sector in accordance with republican principles of mixed government, an essentially conservative reformation could be effected. Simple revolutionary models, in which kings and ancient nobilities were displaced as the symbolic locus of authority by the sovereign people, will be irrelevant. Existing economic, political and ideological elites will be neither overthrown nor liquidated. The power of those who possess economic and cultural capital will be preserved and augmented on condition that it be exercised in the responsible and reflexive manner befitting the citizens of a modern republican polity. The constitutionalisation of the corporation will invest property ownership with a renewed measure of civic and constitutional authority. By the same token, the naked economic power of the bourgeois, either as manager or as investor, must become responsive to the procedural and substantive norms of political discourse and constitutional decision-making. Only the authority of law can hope to subordinate the economic power of capital to the power of reasoned speech.

Law's Aristocratic Republic

The republican reformation of modern civil society will require a paradigm shift in the doctrinal foundation of constitutional and corporate law. Such a transformation in legal consciousness requires the active cooperation of lawyers, judges and legal scholars. Reform of the corporate sector cannot be achieved by treating the legal professions as mere transmission belts for legislative directives handed down from on high. The distinction between law making and law application is not as clear as legal positivists pretend. In the positivist tradition, the objectivity of the law is guaranteed by the formalist model of rules. The orthodox claim to objectivity has always been vulnerable to the realist objection that the application of rules inevitably depends upon subjective judgements. Others, who are neither positivists nor realists, maintain that conventional practices and shared understandings within the legal professions help to constrain the subjective element in the interpretation of law. According to this conventionalist theory, the legal profession is 'a relatively autonomous interpretive community'. Because the legal profession is responsible 'for the shared understandings that shape interpretation', it has 'the power collectively to determine the law's meaning'.[25] Unless the legal professions themselves play a leading role in the republican regeneration of modern civil society, it is difficult to see how either constitutional or corporate law can be weaned away from their doctrinal subservience to both the political theology of sovereignty and the capitalist cult of the divine economy. The interpretive community of legal professionals is itself a sort of shadow corporation exercising governmental and policymaking powers of its own. It too needs to be reconstituted as a little republic.

One response to the conventional power of lawyers is to emphasise 'the anti-democratic quality of legal practice.' According to David Millon, 'the power to determine the law's meaning rests in the hands of the legal profession rather than in the hands of the people's elected representatives'. Conventionalist theory 'reveals that no statute or legal decision can determine its own prospective meaning; meaning derives from interpretation in the context of actual cases as they arise'. Millon denies that 'the decisions that emerge from that process are somehow still public in that they are adequately responsive to, or reflective of, general will or majority preference'. Because no formal mechanisms exist to 'render the profession accountable to the general public for its actions', the actual power of the legal profession stands in contradiction to democratic theory. On this view, unless the interpretive practices of the legal profession can be made subordinate to democratic norms, they cannot be made legitimate. Millon therefore aims to 'democratise' the legal profession by adjusting its ethnic, socio-economic and gender composition to match that of the people at large. In his view, 'a profession that better mirrored the heterogeneity of the general population probably would come closer to reflecting the diversity of the public's values and preferences than the currently constituted profession can do'.[26] Civil society is here conceived as a patchwork of racial, ethnic, religious and lifestyle fiefdoms each entitled to its administratively prescribed share of places in the legal professions.

As we have seen, Millon promotes a similar strategy of refeudalisation in the realm of corporate governance.[27] Shareholders should be relieved of their unique constitutional responsibility for the direction of the firm, while other stakeholders are admitted to a role in the corporate polity commensurate with the functional significance to the enterprise of the resources they control. Millon conceives the legal profession as another sort of corporate entity possessed of its own distinctive jurisgenerative or law making power. For a long time, only white males could share in the exercise of that professional power. Millon identifies a wide range of ethnic, socio-economic and gender interests as potential stakeholders in the law making activities of the legal profession. In both the governance of the corporation and the constitution of the legal profession, Millon's corporatist strategy replaces the citizen with agents empowered to negotiate on behalf of various special interests in a contest among unequals whose outcome is shaped by the claims of money and power.

A more fruitful response to the conventional power of the legal profession would be to recognise it as useful and necessary aristocratic counterpoise to the majoritarian weight of the democratic elements in a modern republican constitution. Over a century and a half ago, Tocqueville observed that lawyers occupied a separate station even in the most democratic society of modern times. In fact, Tocqueville was a pioneer of conventionalist theory. Like Millon, Tocqueville saw that its informal subpolitical role as an interpretive community constituted the legal profession as a real corporate entity, even in the absence of a formal charter from the state. Although 'they naturally constitute *a body*,' it is not 'any previous understanding' or a deliberate 'agreement which directs them to a common end'. The ties are of intellect and predisposition, not of interest and condition. Tocqueville believed that those who devoted themselves to legal pursuits acquired 'from these occupations certain habits of order, a taste for formalities, and a kind of instinctive regard for the regular connection of ideas'. Because 'the analogy of their studies and the uniformity of their proceedings connect their minds together', lawyers 'respond to the constant novelty of human existence in broadly similar ways'.[28] Millon merely restates Tocqueville's insight in the language of academic sociology when he notes that membership 'in the interpretive community involves a commitment to the common interpretive criteria that are internal and specific to the legal profession'.[29]

Both writers agree that the actual law making power of the legal profession cannot easily be justified in terms of democratic principles of popular sovereignty. But their response to the autonomous hermeneutic power of the legal profession is quite different. Millon insists that the legal profession must be made to conform to the requirements of democratic theory even if that means reducing representation to a matter of crude demographic ratios. Tocqueville is not a democratic absolutist for whom the meaning of the law must always mirror the will of the people. Indeed, he saw in the authority of the legal profession 'the most powerful existing security against the excesses of democracy'. That observation did not necessarily imply that the power of the profession was set in perpetual opposition to democracy. In a democratic republic, there was a need for some body of men to play the role assigned to the aristocracy by the classical theory of mixed government. The democracy had to be protected from its own worst instincts. American lawyers constituted 'a sort of privileged body in the scale of intelligence'. Serving as arbiters between their fellow citizens and accustomed to 'directing the blind passions of parties in litigation to their purpose', lawyers were imbued with 'a certain contempt for the judgment of the multitude'.[30] For Tocqueville, the legal profession filled the constitutional vacuum created by the egalitarian spirit of American democracy.

The Republican Reformation of the Legal Profession

While he saw in lawyers a 'portion of the tastes and habits of an aristocracy', Tocqueville denied that they were an alien presence in the democratic body politic. Almost by definition, democratic government 'is favourable to the political power of lawyers.' When kings, lords and property owners were forced to surrender their monopoly on political power, lawyers stepped forward as 'the only men of information and sagacity beyond the sphere of the people, who can be the object of the popular choice'. Because lawyers 'belong to the people by birth and interest' and 'to the aristocracy, by habit and by taste, ... they may be looked upon as the natural bond and connecting link of the two great classes of society'. Far from being set in opposition to democracy, the 'admixture of lawyer-like sobriety with the democratic principle' was essential to the survival of the American republic.[31]

Tocqueville claimed that the 'profession of law is the only aristocratic element which can be amalgamated without violence with the natural elements of democracy, and which can be advantageously and permanently combined with them'.[32] An early nineteenth century French aristocrat can be forgiven for not anticipating the constitutional possibilities opened up by the invention of the dual class capitalisation. Millon has no excuse for not considering the contemporary implications of Tocqueville's work. Unfortunately, Millon never abandons an increasingly threadbare democratic theory in favour of a frank acceptance of the aristocratic role of the legal profession. A republican strategy of constitutional reform would grant formal constitutional recognition to the interpretive community of lawyers, judges and legal scholars. Brought out of the shadowy background, that interpretive community could not only be made accountable to the people at large for its actions, it could develop its own distinctive political style of professional civility.   If lawyers were to achieve constitutional recognition as an aristocracy of intellect and predisposition, they might be more apt to grasp the civic point of reconstituting self-selecting groups of corporate shareholders as a senatorial elite.

The republican reformation of the legal profession could begin by combining the American democratic idea of an elective judiciary with the classical theory of the mixed polity. If the legal profession shares in the production of legal meaning, it should bear formal, public responsibility for the selection of judges in the highest appellate courts. In spelling out the meaning of the law in the most bitterly contested cases, the federal High Court and state or provincial Supreme Courts should be seen to be speaking on behalf of the interpretive communities that they represent. Governments and the people at large have their own obvious and direct interest in the way in which magistrates and district court judges apply more or less settled understandings of the law to disputes over the facts of a particular matter. At the lowest level of the judicial hierarchy, governments and the people at large can usefully exercise the sovereign prerogative in the selection of judges. As for the high courts, the power of election should devolve to the legal professions.   Lawyers can accept corporate responsibility for the constitution of legal meaning only if they are liberated from the constitutional limitations imposed by the absolutist doctrines of parliamentary and popular sovereignty.   Some such *Freisetzung* of professional agency from statist constitutional structures is essential if the legal profession is to play a creative role in the republican reformation of civil society.

This is not to suggest that the legal profession should become a law unto itself. High Court judges should have their tenure confirmed or denied by the people at large after having served between five and ten years in office. Some might fear that such a confirmation procedure would allow a benighted populace to eliminate progressive judges who offend against populist prejudices. But, if such a judge enjoyed widespread support within the legal profession, he could be returned to office by his professional peers who would then be compelled to defend their action in the court of public opinion. In this way, both the professional few and the democratic many would play a direct role in the constitution of the judiciary.[33]

Democrats such as Millon, worry about 'the legal profession's power to determine the law's meaning,' since it 'offends the notion of self-government that lies at the heart of the traditional rule of law ideal'. In his view, not even the popular election of judges would curb the anti-democratic impact of professional power. The interpretive activity of judges, in those American states where they are elected, rather than appointed, still occurs 'within the larger context of the legal profession's shared understanding'. Millon believes that popularly elected judges are 'probably more likely to conform their interpretation to professional understandings ("what the law requires") than to perceived dictates of popular preference'.[34] Determined to subordinate that autonomous professional authority to the constitutional hegemony of the demos, Millon aims to tailor the demographic composition of the legal profession to match that of the people at large.

In order to 'democratise' legal interpretation, the legal profession must mirror 'the heterogeneity of the general population'. Electing judges is not enough to 'alter the terms on which the legal profession's interpretive conversations are conducted'. Constitutional orthodoxy tells us that these conversations must be conducted in democratic terms or not at all. If its interpretive activity is to be legitimate, the values and preferences shaping legal decisions (and non-decisions) must be brought 'closer to reflecting the diversity of the public's values and preferences than the currently constituted profession can do'.[35] That the legal profession might be entitled and even obliged to develop its own, quite possibly aristocratic, predispositions is out of the question for the democratic absolutist.

Even though the sovereign people do not require the consent of any other human agent to make law,[36] Millon might be puzzled to find himself labelled an absolutist. After all, he claims that 'democracy is a system for maximising the range of debate and deliberation about normative questions rather than a mechanism for faithful registration of the majority's preselected preferences'. His 'assumption is that a richer mix of participants will generate a richer mix of normative outlooks'. Millon's 'solution to the problem of legislative legitimacy' emphasises the value of what he calls 'conversational pluralism'.[37] He hopes that by incorporating an officially prescribed spectrum of racial, gender and socio-economic groupings within the legal profession, legal discourse will be opened up to a greater diversity of views.

But, by reducing democratic theory to the politics of identity, Millon would change the face of corporate and professional power, not its nature. A republican strategy of constitutional reform would aim instead to reconstitute the internal political order of both the state and the corporate sector. The political and constitutional struggle provoked by such a movement would be much more likely to generate a fruitful diversity of views than yet another bureaucratic scheme to specify the ethnicity, gender or socio-economic origins of those permitted to occupy the established seats of public, professional and corporate power.

One, Two, Many Little Republics

Despite the increasingly multicultural complexion of Anglo-American civilisation, political and constitutional debate remains confined within extremely narrow limits. No obvious alternative to a corporate welfare state powered by a globalised society of perpetual growth is on public offer. Neither affirmative action in legal education and professional employment, nor stakeholder laws in the realm of corporate governance, will upset the bedrock realities of autonomous corporate and professional power. That free floating, discretionary power can become constitutionally legitimate only if public spheres are created within the powerful corporate and professional bodies that now function as private fiefdoms.

A democratic theory still wedded to the constitutional assumptions appropriate to the era of simple modernisation will never solve the problems of corporate and professional legitimacy as they arise in risk society. In fact, democratic theory made matters worse by refusing to acknowledge the legitimacy of Tocqueville's legal aristocracy. Judges and lawyers came to play a central role in the state of courts and parties that soon came to dominate American political life. At the same time, Jacksonian democrats launched their assault on the aristocratic pretensions of the legal profession by aiming to ensure that any male citizen who was free, white and twenty-one could become a lawyer.[38] Meanwhile, the legal profession as a whole was effectively privatised within the overwhelmingly bourgeois domain of civil society. It was not long before American lawyers lost their Tocquevillean resemblance to a natural aristocracy. By the late nineteenth century, the commanding heights of the legal profession were occupied by a thoroughly commercialised corporate bar.[39] By constituting new public spaces within the legal profession and endowing it with new constitutional responsibilities, the almost complete embourgeoisement of the legal profession might be at least partially reversed.

By investing lawyers, legal scholars and sitting judges with the constitutional authority to select the judges for the highest courts in the land, it might be possible to trigger a republican chain reaction. Judges elected by their professional peers could become a vanguard element in the reflexive modernisation of the bourgeois liberal republic. Lawyers would possess their own parcel of sovereignty. But the parcellisation of sovereignty would proceed in accordance with republican principles rather than feudal precedents. Conscious of their professional responsibility for the constitution of the judiciary, lawyers could choose to act more like a civic aristocracy of intellect and predispositions and less like a coterie of bourgeois insiders whose main business is to protect the interests and well-being of a rich and powerful corporate clientele.

By the early twentieth century, the Tocquevillean ideal of the lawyer as thinly disguised aristocrat was displaced by 'the image of the leading lawyer as a skilled negotiator and facilitator, the practical man of business'.[40] As professional servants of corporate power, lawyers earned a well deserved reputation for legal legerdemain. One of the great doctrinal achievements of the nineteenth century American corporate lawyer came with judicial recognition of the corporation as a real entity entitled to all the constitutional rights, privileges and immunities guaranteed by the Constitution to natural persons.[41] That professional struggle to defend corporate interests by all available legal means continues with recent judicial decisions recognising corporate rights to free speech or free expression. Corporate rights to finance political campaigns, broadcast political advertising or promote particular products have all been held to be constitutionally protected freedoms.[42] The courts that have been so solicitous in their concern for the constitutional rights of big business corporations have been slower to spell out the corporate responsibilities attached to their de facto status as private governments. A bourgeois legal profession has worked to guarantee every corporation's right to life, liberty and property. Lawyers with a more refined sense of civic responsibility will be needed to carve out public spaces within the corporate and professional associations of modern civil society wherein the bourgeois can learn to be a republican and act as a citizen.

The interpretive community of lawyers and judges will become more sympathetic to the constitutionalisation of the corporation once it has been itself constituted as a civil body politic performing the functions of an electoral college. Certainly a republican programme of reflexive modernisation will never be achieved without the active cooperation of legal professionals. The same observation applies to media corporations. Given their special role in the contemporary practice of responsible government, media corporations should be, as I have argued, among the first to be governed by a politically responsible body of active investors meeting on a plane of political equality. Only if the political model of the corporation functions well in the media industry should it be extended more generally. The way is already open to a republican legal profession to spell out the civic implications of the doctrine that the freedom to broadcast political advertising is a necessary incident of representative democracy. One might reasonably infer that media corporations invoking the freedom of expression essential to the constitutional integrity of the bourgeois liberal republic should govern themselves in accordance with republican norms of civic freedom and political responsibility. The paradox here is that the unrestricted freedom of political broadcasting can itself trivialise, degrade and corrupt the political process. But to deny corporate rights to free speech is to abandon the political model of the modern business corporation.[43]

The standard leftist response to this dilemma invokes the idea of democracy to justify the legislative regulation of corporate and commercial speech. According to Allan Hutchinson, 'the regulation of commercial speech must be placed firmly in the hands of the democratic process and not placed beyond their reach by the courts in the name of constitutional wisdom'.[44] This position is based on two assumptions. The first assumption is that there is an inherent conflict between democracy and the judicial protection of constitutional rights. The second assumption is that the business corporation cannot be treated in law as an association of responsible individuals capable of exercising and deserving the protection of the constitutional rights available to natural persons.

Hutchinson considers judicial review undemocratic because the decisions of a popularly elected legislature may be overturned by judges who are unelected and unaccountable. He and others also reject the notion of a constitutional right to corporate free speech on the grounds that the personality 'of a business corporation is less authentic than that of other organisational entities'. The 'voice' of the modern business corporation 'represents not a plurality and unity of people or citizens, but a plurality and unity of capital'.[45] Having made such assumptions, Hutchinson concludes that there are only two alternatives when it comes to the 'crucial issue' of 'who or what is to regulate' commercial speech. If universal speech is not subject to control by 'the citizenry and consumers at large, through various legislative measures and regulative agencies', it will be left to 'the commercial sector of the economy in the name of the market'. A third way depends on neither the state nor the market.[46] This republican strategy would open up new public spaces for citizens in both the corporate sector and the state.

Unless the modern business corporation is constitutionalised, technological development will continue to serve the narrowly instrumental goals of profit and power. Technology has 'become a political force of the first magnitude, permanently transforming all aspects of life'. Corporate control over the process of innovation allows technology 'to run wild in a way that threatens our freedom and our very lives'. In the risk society, 'we find ourselves confronting worlds of our own making - mistakes, uncertainties and catastrophes for which neither God not nature, however defined, can be held responsible'. As a matter of survival, we must 'install a steering mechanism and brakes in a scientific/technological civilisation that tends to rush full speed ahead, unleashing explosive powers in the process'.[47] Under the present regime, nobody can be held responsible for these developments. If it did nothing else, the republican reformation of the corporate sector would help to slow the decision-making process down to the point where responsible parties can be observed, identified and made liable.

As an alternative to the current system of 'organised irresponsibility', Ulrich Beck proposes an 'upper house of technology' in which ethicists, politicians, the public, lay persons and technological experts alter the prevailing norms governing the implementation of new technologies. At present, corporate decision-making takes place 'in the twilight zone where politics, science and industry meet'. In order for scientists, technologists and ordinary citizens to break free from their bondage to industry, new institutional forms and 'occasions for public debate on different technologies must be created'.[48] Beck's council of technology could be built into the governance of the business corporation by employing dual class capital structures to create a model of the civil body politic adapted to the risk society. But any movement to apply a republican canon of institutional design to the subpolitical realm of corporate power will have to overcome the tremendous weight of institutional and intellectual inertia that confines constitutional discourse within its accustomed channels.

Beyond the Left-Right Dichotomy

The republican reformation of Anglo-American civil society would entail a radical transformation in the terms of political discourse. Throughout the long age of the democratic revolution, public life has been dominated by an ideological conflict between the Left and the Right. Nowadays, the division between the two positions seems blurred and irrelevant. 'The Right has lost its main enemy: communism. The Left has chosen to collaborate with its own: capitalism'. Having long since committed itself to uncontrolled capitalist development, the Right's defence of the traditional values of family, patriotism and authority has been confused, hypocritical and ineffective. So long as the 'best people' devote themselves to 'justifying the whims of the richest', it is 'impossible to distinguish between a genuine aristocracy and a so-called "elite" defined exclusively by money'. The Right sets itself up as the champion of spiritual and traditional values against the corrosive power of leftist materialism but serves corporate and professional elites 'whose sole reason for being is economic activity'. Having allied itself with wealth, the Right, 'contributed more than the Left to the destruction of the values which it pretended to advocate'.[49]

For its part, the Left defined itself in opposition to the market economy and private property once it succeeded in its prolonged assault on the traditional authority of kings, nobles and priests. A planned, centralised and state-controlled economy was to replace the capitalist mode of production. But neither socialists nor communists challenged the central objective of the capitalist economy: constant growth. Keynesian economics and the rise of mass consumerism undermined the capacity of the Left to rally its supporters by proposing 'to change society'. As the Left was corrupted by prosperity, it 'contributed more than the Right to prevent the advent of the new society it wished to bring about'. The result has been a shift towards the centre. Those on the Left and the Right now 'worship the same god: the cult of performance, efficiency and profit'. As long established political divisions crumble, leaders in both camps insist that the iron laws of market efficiency and the unlimited growth of technology are ineluctable features of modern life. The outcomes of capitalist development are not a matter of choice. Politics has therefore been reduced 'to a simple technique of administrative management'. Even the Left has 'put the freedom of capital before the freedom of citizens, and has laid its statist identity to rest without, however trying to recentre itself in society'.[50]

The recent discovery of civil society might seem to belie the claim that 'progressives' have forsworn their statist predilections only to embrace the lordship of capital. Andrew Arato and Jean Cohen, for example, offer their 'self-reflexive model of civil society' as a contribution to the revitalisation of democratic political theory. Acknowledging that the survival of civil society is endangered by the instrumental logic of administrative and economic mechanisms, they nevertheless maintain that the sphere of social interaction standing between the economy and the state should become 'the primary locus for the potential expansion of democracy' in the bourgeois liberal republic. Unlike 'the actors of political and economic society', civil society is not 'directly involved with state power and economic production'. According to this schema, civil society represents a socio-cultural lifeworld surrounded by the expanding domain of the corporate welfare state. Civil society is 'composed above all of the intimate sphere (especially the family), the sphere of associations (especially voluntary associations), social movements and forms of public communication'. According to Arato and Cohen, the expansion of civil society could further democracy, not through the direct control or conquest of state power, but through 'the generation of influence through the life of democratic associations and unconstrained discussion in the cultural public sphere'. Similarly, civil society exerts influence on the corporate economy through 'the legalisation of trade unions, collective bargaining, co-determination and so on'.[51]

Arato and Cohen's vision of a self-limiting civil society pays lip service to traditional republican values but, in the final analysis, fails to challenge the refeudalisation of the corporate welfare state. Their appeal to the politics of influence is neo-feudal since it presupposes the permanent primacy of the corporate barons and political princes who finally determine who gets what, where, when and how. By locating civil society outside and apart from both the state and the corporate sector, Arato and Cohen effectively limit the scope of a republican strategy focused on the constitutional reformation of civil society. On their account, neither the internal political order of the state nor the governance of the big business corporation can be reconstituted in accordance with the citizenship principle. At most, the state and the corporate sector can be made more sensitive to 'the requirements of the external environment'.[52] Civil society influences state and corporate decision-makers in a process of bargaining and negotiation between groups varying widely in wealth, status and power. Civil society serves as a sort of built-in curb finder for the benevolent New Class of technocrats, managers and intellectuals whose job it is to steer the sprawling behemoth of the corporate welfare state into the era of reflexive modernity.

Arato and Cohen do want to further the cause of the democratic revolution ignited during the age of enlightenment. They warn 'that democratic revolutions can remain democratic only if they institutionalise civil society'. But the democratic utopia of civil society can be realised only if it observes strict limits on the possibilities of civic action. Arato and Cohen insist that the utopian project of civil society 'is one of differentiation rather than unification'. That is to say, the boundaries separating civil from political and economic society will be respected. So too will the established powers and prerogatives of our political and economic elites. What they persist in calling the 'utopian horizon of civil society' can be reached only through 'the reflexive continuation of the welfare state'.[53] In their own distinctive fashion, Arato and Cohen continue the grand centrist tradition of American political science. They urge their readers to accept the established structures of political and economic power, not just as an ineluctable given, but as the best of all possible worlds.

In their 'progressive' project, the task of theory is not to point the way to a revolutionary rupture with the established order.   Rather, Arato and Cohen aim to defend the lifeworld of civil society against further colonisation by the political and economic subsystems of the corporate welfare state.   By uncovering the distinctive logics of political power and economic rationalism, they hope to identify the limits within which effective economic, political and social action can occur.   Arato and Cohen want to disabuse us of the notion that the sorts of political action and democratic decision-making found in civil society can be carried over into the domain of political and economic society.   Free association and communicative interaction may be the constitutive principles of civil society but Arato and Cohen are adamant that the state and the economy are ruled by power and money.   In the state and the economy, strategic and instrumental behaviour take priority over the norms of communicative interaction.

This is not to say that democracy, citizenship and publicity have no place in the internal workings of the state and the corporate sector.   Rather, their 'central thesis' is 'that democracy can go much further on the level of civil society than on the level of political or economic society, because here the coordinating mechanism of communicative interaction has fundamental priority'.   In the modern bourgeois liberal republic, civil society can outfit individuals, families and voluntary associations with the legal, civil and political rights necessary to organise themselves into public spaces with the capacity to influence those who operate through the impersonal media of money and power.   But democratic forms such as consumer and producer cooperatives, trade unions and co-determination are possible within the economic sector only 'up to the point where efficient steering is threatened'. To those who long for more extensive forms of economic democracy, Arato and Cohen offer little consolation.   When it comes to the economy, they say, 'the requirements of efficiency and market rationality can be disregarded in the name of democracy only at the cost of both'.[54]   Neither democracy nor the free market offers much scope for civic action.   Left and Right now see both as 'learned behaviours' in our collective adaptation to the requirements of political and economic modernity.   Civil society as the realm of freedom is conditioned on grim acceptance of its necessary limits.

The Limits on Civil Society: The Progressive Version

Republican jurisprudence should take a more expansionist approach to the institutional boundaries of civil society.   It could do so by seeking to reclaim some of the sociocultural terrain already colonised by political and economic institutions. For republicans, civil society is a goal, not a datum. Arato and Cohen, by contrast, set out with 'the obviously plausible counter thesis' that the bourgeois liberal republics of the advanced Western world already possess 'civil societies, however imperfect'.[55] They have no apparent confidence that civil society could develop to the point where it could begin to counter-colonise the territory of its state and corporate overlords.

In Arato and Cohen's political cosmology, citizens talk but they rarely act. Citizenship is conceived in terms of communicative interaction. A republican jurisprudence would recognise as well the expressive dimension of citizenship. It is of course true that citizens inhabit a discursive space of communicative interaction. But the public spaces of the republic also provide a dramatic setting where noble and courageous deeds can be performed. Even the iron laws of economic efficiency and political powers invoked by Arato and Cohen to keep civil society in its place could be challenged by a new breed of corporate citizens determined to master the play of economic and political fortune. If civil society is indeed as much of an unrealised aspiration as an accomplished reality, citizens must somehow be moved to achieve their civilising goals through concerted civic and political action.

Arato and Cohen's theory of civil society reflects the prevalent sense of resignation before the all-powerful 'realities' of global capitalism. Anyone who hopes to find in Arato and Cohen's 'utopian' vision of civil society an outlet for their agonistic longing to perform great deeds will more likely be plunged into a fit of melancholy. The scope for heroic action in modern society is strictly limited. In both the state and the economy, the expressive needs of the individual are routinely subordinated to the strategic and instrumental requirements of the system. Arato and Cohen counsel us to remember that the need for the steering mechanisms of money and power 'must be respected if we expect them to function efficiently'.[56] It has been said that '*the inability to act is itself the cause of melancholy*'.[57] When one discovers that not even the 'utopian horizon of civil society' offers much scope for action, one is bound to be a bit depressed. On Arato and Cohen's theory, the republican reformation of Anglo-American civil society would not take us much further than the familiar achievements of Scandinavian and German social democracy: collective bargaining, co-determination and perhaps representative workers' councils along with greater encouragement for consumer and producer cooperatives.

Together with Gunther Teubner, Arato and Cohen propose reforms in corporate governance designed to install more effective 'receptors' for influences emanating from civil society. Expressed in the language of systems theory, their goal is to get the 'optimal balancing of performance and function by taking into account the requirements of the external environment'.[58] In Teubner's elaboration of this programme, the function of 'receptor' or 'guidance mechanism' may be performed by managerial personnel. Teubner believes that the constitutional requirements of reflexive modernisation can be satisfied so long as corporate managers are subject to duties of disclosure, undergo regular audits and carry a duty of cooperation requiring them to bargain with stakeholders in good faith. Like any feudal lord, corporate managers may be bound to consult regularly with organised interests inside and outside the enterprise. More generally, managers in every large-scale organisation, whether corporate, governmental or military, will 'be made responsible for creating a system of coordination, supervision, monitoring and control'.[59]

This is a far cry from the republican reformation of the corporate sector. Having accepted state and corporate power as institutional givens, the neo-feudal model of reflexive modernity reduces democracy to a problem of communication. Like Paul Hirst's neo-pluralist programme of associative democracy, the concept of civil society favoured by Arato, Cohen and Teubner remains tied to a behaviourist model of accountability. If 'progressive' reforms are to be achievable, they must be premised on the hard-nosed, realist assumption that people 'are rational pursuers of their own interests'. In just that spirit, Hirst advocates a decentralised, associational commonwealth to be constructed on the terrain marked out by Arato and Cohen's civil society. Once again, civil society is permitted to provide a democratic supplement to the otherwise unaccountable structures of political and economic society. Hirst portrays democracy as an effective mode of 'governance based upon an adequate flow of information from governed to governors, and the coordination of the implementation of policy through ongoing consultation with those affected by it'.[60]

In the domain of corporate governance Hirst, too, leans towards a neo-feudal solution. For years, Hirst has denied that company organisation bears any resemblance to a 'republic of shareholders governed by their elected representatives'.[61] Not even workers can claim uncontested primacy within a corporate polity. Effective communication within an enterprise requires a recognition 'that there are more stakeholders in industry than just the immediate producers'. To enhance the role of stakeholders is to deny the relevance of the citizenship principle to corporate governance. Hirst frankly proclaims that his scheme of associational democracy does not require citizens; it can survive on the 'assumption of narrowly self-interested behaviour' on the part of every member of every voluntary association in civil society. Shareholders are just another special interest group along with managers, employers, customers and creditors.[62]

Communicative interaction between shareholders and other stakeholders will create a new sort of economic partnership, not a new model of the civil body politic. Arato and Cohen stress that the point of conceiving democracy as communication 'is not to increase participation as an end in itself, nor should the results be judged by this standard'. Instead, a reflexive corporate law would develop a level and type of participation that would make institutions 'sensitive to the outside effects of the internal attempts to maximise internal rationality'. Arato and Cohen emphasise the economic limits on political action. They suggest that reforms designed to enhance the reflexivity of corporate governance 'must observe the limits of economic rationality - profitability in particular - by producing profit and investment levels within the range of functionally equivalent organisational solutions'.[63] What this would mean in practice is the sort of legislative and judicial support for stakeholder interests already available in some jurisdictions in the advanced capitalist world. Hirst, too, takes pains to soothe any fears that associative democracy might entail a revolutionary break with corporate capitalism. He assures his readers that his reformed model of corporate governance amounts to 'little more than an amalgam of Japanese and German best practice and would not in [itself] render firms uncompetitive'.[64]

The Limits on Civil Society: The Conservative Version

The differences between progressives and conservatives on matters of corporate governance are 'ones of degree, not of kind'. Both camps agree that the corporate sector is driven primarily by the economic logic of efficiency. To civil society is left the task of generating the trust and mutual interdependence without which market relationships would be impossible to sustain. Conservatives may insist that the corporation is best understood as a nexus of contracts but they also deny that Economic Man is 'driven by purely pecuniary incentives'. Their 'rational choice theory encompasses all incentives to which humans respond, including such things as risk aversion and even a generalised sense of fairness'. The autonomous individual seeking to maximise his satisfactions must be embedded in a real moral and social order. Conflict arises between conservative contractarians and progressive corporatists whenever the state intervenes in economic society to impose 'mandatory codes of honourable and trustworthy conduct'. Progressives now 'favour a drastic expansion of corporate law's regulatory jurisdiction to encompass mandatory rules governing the relationships between the corporation and its various non-shareholder constituencies'. Conservatives contend that corporate law is and should remain a body 'of default rules, from which shareholders are free to depart'.[65]

Bainbridge invokes 'the principle of sphere sovereignty' to justify the autonomy of the corporate sector. In his view, progressives are too eager to promote 'state intrusion into the private sphere in the name of some communal good'. As we have seen, Millon and other progressives 'posit that corporations have obligations to employees and other non-shareholder constituencies that extend beyond mere contractual obligation'. If trust and mutual interdependence do not ensure the performance of those obligations, progressives are prepared to enlist the state to serve as a 'coercive backstop'. But progressives have learned from the failure of bureaucratic socialism. 'Instead of economic power being exercised directly by the central government, state control would be dispersed throughout the economy'. Stakeholder constituencies would be incorporated into the governance structure of corporate enterprises.   Conservatives claim that this communitarian corporation nationalises 'people instead of companies as individuals are subsumed by their officially designated communities'.[66]   In their stock reply to such accusations, progressives portray stakeholder groups, not as mere creatures of the state, but as real entities whose interests must be factored into the corporate decision-making process.

Both camps recognise that a civil society of families, churches and other voluntary associations can and must exercise influence on both government and the corporate sector. Social networks of trust and mutual interdependence provide the social capital necessary to sustain individuals in the pursuit of money and power within the economic and political realms.[67] Conservatives insist, however, 'that moral life consists mainly of the habitual *private* exercise of truthfulness, courage, justice, mercy, and the other virtues'. The state's role must therefore be 'limited to that of a facilitator of private gain-seeking through provision of default rules'. Bainbridge worries that 'America is becoming a low-virtue society ... precisely because of the sort of statism the stakeholderists propose to foist upon us in the name of trust.'[68]

But one is entitled to wonder how the unrestrained growth of corporate capitalism will somehow regenerate a high-virtue society. Bainbridge concedes that the modern business corporation itself does little to inculcate virtue. On the contrary, the big corporations 'in fact resemble the nanny state - a large impersonal bureaucracy with the power to terrorise, but no ability to nurture'. Like Arato and Cohen, conservative contractarians believe that the media of money and power must draw on the spiritual resources of the lifeworld. Bainbridge declares 'that religious communities are critical to the creation of a virtuous citizenry'. Religious faith becomes the cement of social order. We are more likely to act virtuously when we believe 'in an external power higher and more permanent than the state, who is aware of [our] shortcomings' and who will hold us to account in the hereafter. But churches are but one of the many voluntary communities that provide 'a cloud of witnesses about whom we care and whose good opinion we value, thus encouraging us to strive to comport ourselves in accordance with communal norms'. It is true that the corporation exists to maximise wealth, not as a school of the civic virtues, but Bainbridge takes comfort in the fact that a corporate enterprise 'may harbour within it sub-groups that amount to communities of shared values'. He acknowledges that the host of collective action problems plaguing shareholders, creditors and customers precludes these groups 'from developing any sense of community'. Nevertheless 'those who work for the corporation may be able to form true communities'.[69]

Bainbridge takes a very rosy view of modern corporate culture when he asserts that one's 'co-workers thus provide precisely the cloud of witnesses so essential to the inculcation of civic virtue'.[70] But unchecked managerial power could easily undermine a 'true community' of co-workers in the absence of a state-sponsored system of collective bargaining. The world of corporate managers themselves, whatever the situation of their subordinates, gives little cause for optimism about the ethos shared by those who work for the big corporations. Robert Jackall claims that 'at bottom, a great deal of managerial work consists of ongoing struggles for dominance and status'. Success depends upon the 'socially recognised ability to work one's will, to get one's way ... in both the petty and large choices of organisational life'. In a corporate bureaucracy, what matters is not what a person 'believes or says but how well he has mastered the ideologies and rhetorics that serve his corporation; not what he stands for but whom he stands with in the labyrinths of his organisation'.[71] This is not a pretty picture.

In fact, a cloud of witnesses among corporate executives all too easily turns into a conspiracy of silence. Standing by one's actions becomes less important than avoiding blame. Jackall concludes that the ethos fashioned by corporate managers 'turns principles into guidelines, ethics into etiquette, values into tasks, personal responsibility into adroitness at public relations, and notions of truth into credibility'. Managerial elites clearly play a 'pivotal institutional role in our epoch'. As an 'unintended consequence of their personal striving', corporate managers help create 'a society where morality becomes indistinguishable from the quest for one's survival and advantage.'[72]

Bainbridge could concede that the corporation creates 'for managers an intricate set of moral mazes that are paradigmatic of the quandaries of public life in our social order.'[73] He nevertheless denies that the state has any solutions to offer. Our best hope still lies with the churches and other voluntary communities with virtue-instilling functions which would be undermined by state interference. Conservatives portray the autonomy of the corporate sector as a bulwark sheltering the seedbeds of virtue in civil society. The corporation is another 'intermediary institution standing between the individual and Leviathan'. Tyranny, in this conservative view, is more likely to come from the state than from the private sector. Conservatives insist that, so long as private property is protected from state control, freedom can survive. But 'separate property from private possession and Leviathan becomes master of all'.[74]

Conservatives turn a blind eye to the abolition of private property through the separation of ownership and control in the modern business corporation. That is because they also prefer to forget that dominion over property once carried political responsibilities. Separate property ownership from political responsibility and Mammon becomes master of all. Modern corporate culture 'creates for managers a Calvinist world without a Calvinist God, a world marked with the same profound anxiety that characterised the old Protestant ethic but one stripped of that ideology's comforting illusions'.[75] In a disenchanted world, the divine economy becomes the external power punishing us whenever we stray from its commandments. John Ralston Saul marvels at the 'literally Old Testament approach to public debt' preached by the managerial class. 'The sin. The terrible shame of having sinned against the god of prudence. The need to atone, to suffer for having had it too easy'. Economists and managers have become high priests in a cult of endless growth and their 'only job is to uncover the divine plan' for profits and prosperity. Because they do not create and cannot stop that plan, managerial elites exercise power without responsibility.[76]

Corporate Property and Civic Virtue

Conservatives can be depended upon to resist the expansion of the state 'beyond those functions prescribed by custom and convention'. But they have been remarkably indifferent to the anarchic and morally corrosive impact of capitalist development. After all, it is not just the nanny state that has overturned every mode of life 'legitimised by ancient usage'. Consumer capitalism too is 'perpetually grasping at new aspects of social life to drag into its slavering maw'.[77] The nanny state and corporate capitalism are two sides of a coin minted by the managerial revolution. Both public and private sectors are governed by managerial elites that civil society may influence but never control.

That managerial regime is the fruit of the ongoing revolt of propertied elites against the responsibilities of rulership. Progressives claim that state-mandated reforms will make the managerial class accountable for their behaviour. Conservatives counter that society will be better off if individuals are left free to pursue their own interests. Neither side sees any relationship between property ownership and the civic virtues. We need to restore the connection between property and virtue in the corporate sector. Civil society must not be left to the tender mercies of an unreformed corporate sector. Progressives and conservatives now serve as publicists for rival empires. While progressives promote the state, conservatives back the corporate sector in the race to colonise civil society. Both imperial powers exploit and despoil the spiritual resources of the lifeworld to fuel their own expansion.

Bainbridge assures us that conservative contractarians will allow 'Tory principles to trump economic analysis'. In the past, Tories believed that 'custom, convention and old prescription are checks both upon man's anarchic impulse and upon the innovator's lust for power'.[78] Apparently, contemporary conservatism believes that the lust for economic gain can be squared with the prescriptive authority of custom once we become fully dependent upon the corporate system for our very survival. Others are bound to distinguish between mass addiction to a high-intensity culture of consumption and a decent respect for tradition.

Bainbridge seems to have little or no respect for the accumulated historical experience of mankind before the advent of 'democratic capitalism' in the United States. He approves the destruction of 'arbitrary class distinctions' through the enhanced personal and social mobility fostered by the growth of the corporate system.[79] If class distinctions are arbitrary simply because they rest upon custom and ancient usage, all traditions, values and ways of life are open to destruction at the hands of those who manage the corporate economy. In the face of a corporate system hooked on perpetual innovation, the survival of civil society depends upon its capacity to spawn a natural aristocracy able to shoulder responsibility for the fate of the republic. Whatever one thinks of the age-old distinction between aristocracy and the commons, it was not always arbitrary. By suppressing the distinctive roles of the few and the many, democratic capitalism has upset the constitutional balance.

If civil society is to gain control over the risks of capitalist development, something more than influence over political and economic society is required. Citizens must carve out their own constitutional role in the spheres of sovereign authority allocated to the state and the corporate sector respectively. For starters, the informal interpretive community of lawyers and legal scholars, along with the people at large, should rise out of civil society to wrest control over judicial appointments away from the Crown. The judiciary can never be independent of government until the artificial reason of the law becomes the intellectual property of an autonomous civil society. An elective judiciary could combine with shareholder senates to compete with managerial power in both the public and private sectors. Political competition poses more of an obstacle to the expansion of the corporate welfare state than the black-letter text of a written constitution. Unless the judiciary arises out of a voluntary community of lawyers and legal scholars enjoying public confidence, it will remain 'part and parcel of the government apparatus whose powers they are supposed to limit'. That being so, there is precious little reason why supreme court judges should 'want to constrain the power of the very organisation that provides them with jobs, money and prestige'.[80] Much the same could be said of the various independent directors, auditors, institutional investors and other watchdogs set in place to monitor managerial performance in the corporate sector. Relying upon one set of managers to watch another will do little to limit the power or the self-serving ambitions of the managerial regime. Failure to constitute shareholder senates as independent loci of civic authority will leave the corporate sector in the hands of managerial elites upon whom states and societies have become dependent for employment and revenues. This is a recipe for neo-feudalism.

The alternative is a republican model of corporate governance. We face a constitutional choice between feudalism and federalism. A republican form of government now requires the extension of the federal principle into the corporate sector. Both federalism and feudalism recognise the principle of sphere sovereignty. According to Bainbridge, sphere sovereignty sees society consisting 'of multiple entities - such as the state, churches, families and corporations - each having a distinct identity'. Under the neo-feudal dispensation, the state would have 'no right to interfere with the internal government of such entities outside its sovereign sphere'.[81] In a federal polity, by contrast, both the state and the corporate sector would be subject to a constitutional guarantee of republican government.

When corporate neo-feudalism can be promoted in the 'progressive' language of academic leftism, while 'conservatives' champion the uncontrolled expansion of corporate capitalism, we may reasonably speak of a crisis in democratic theory. To deal with that crisis, we should return to the first principles of republican government. As we have seen, the ancient ideal of the mixed polity could play an important role in the reflexive modernisation of the contemporary corporate welfare state. The ownership of corporate property could become not just the material foundation for new forms of corporate citizenship but also the institutional medium for the practice of the civic virtues. Property ownership could acquire a coherent and legitimate constitutional role in the era of reflexive corporatism that it could never sustain under the electoral reign of good King Demos.

Property was conceived by Blackstone as a form of absolute dominion over the external things of the world.[82] In the days when property was a relationship between a person and a thing, landed property, in particular, provided citizens with the leisured independence necessary to rise out of the private domain of necessity into the public realm of civic freedom. The public sphere was both a discursive space and a dramatic setting. The actors on the political stage need to cultivate the virtues and skills appropriate to whatever roles they seek or find to play. In an age when even contract was assimilated into property law, rights over things, in and of themselves, offered little scope for the exercise of the civic virtues. Despite the importance of civic virtue to the English Commonwealth tradition, there was 'no known way of representing virtue as a right'.[83] Unlike the concept of *jus* in natural jurisprudence, virtue has to do with a relation between persons. It does not denote a relationship between persons and things. Nowadays, property in corporate shares establishes a relation between persons each claiming a share in the wealth generated by a joint enterprise. The question is whether any of those persons have individual or corporate rights to cultivate and practice the civic virtues.

In the modern context of corporate governance, virtue would not signify merely 'a disposition to righteousness'. Rather in a 'strictly political sense, it becomes a quality of the relations between persons equal in citizenship and between them and the republic, *polis* or vivere civile'. Virtue is a quality that emerges out of the relationship of equality established between the members of a body politic. Property used to be 'the pre-condition of virtue, but not the medium' in which it was expressed. Civic virtue might 'entail the presence of all manner of rights, but it was neither necessary nor appropriate to premise a right in order to explain its presence'.[84] But, now that property has expanded to include almost any sort of legal claim, both rights and virtue are grounded in relations between persons. Under these circumstances, it is not unreasonable to conceive a constitutional doctrine guaranteeing the right of shareholders to a form of corporate governance serving as a school of the civic virtues for those prepared to heed its lessons.

When England was an 'open aristocracy, based on property and patronage',[85] the parliamentary body politic was notorious for its corruption. Property, especially landed property, was the indispensable qualification for entry into the public realm. In the settler dominions there were sporadic efforts to use property qualifications as a mechanism of selection for upper chambers designed to serve as a surrogate for the aristocratic House of Lords.[86] Property ownership lost its special constitutional status when it became evident that the open invasion of the public realm by propertied interests led to wholesale corruption. So long as property ownership was a qualification for membership in the political nation, it was practically impossible for the citizen or the bourgeois to keep his private property interests separate from his public role in the state.[87] But now the public interest as represented by shareholder senates could colonise the quintessentially bourgeois realm of corporate governance. The active investor could become civil society's answer to the corporate bagmen who have hollowed out the legitimacy of the bourgeois liberal republic by subordinating politics to the cult of economic growth. It is no secret that many 'corporations remain autocracies, and some can be tyrannies for their employees, regulating every aspect of their lives'.[88] Those who presently control those corporations should be made responsible to and through a shareholder senate comprised of active investors, each possessed of a substantial private stake in the joint enterprise. That can never happen as long as we pay heed only to those who deny both our capacity and our need to resist the lordship of capital.

The republican reformation of corporate governance will not deprive stakeholder groups of influence in the decision-making processes of the modern business enterprise. On the contrary, shareholder senates would stimulate new forms of political action within and outside the corporation. Shareholders would have a recognised responsibility to act so as to control corporate behaviour. Stakeholders could lobby active investors to consider third party interests when exercising their corporate franchise. Some investors in some firms might resist stakeholder influence on matters of pressing public concern. Such recalcitrance might invite populist retribution through state action. In other words, the reinvention of aristocracy might spur the democracy to reassert itself. At the very least, the governors of the corporate sector would be brought out of the shadows and given a human face. Once they step into their new role, shareholder senates will become public repositories of civic authority. Should active investors rebel in the name of the common world against the irresponsible exercise of managerial power that reservoir of political legitimacy will be replenished with a flow of public good will.

Notes

1   Guy Debord, *Society of the Spectacle* (Detroit: Black and Red, 1970); Ernest Gellner, *Nations and Nationalism* (Oxford: Blackwell, 1983).

2   Ulrich Beck, 'The Reinvention of Politics' in Ulrich Beck, *et al, Reflexive Modernisation: Politics, Tradition and Aesthetics in the Modern Social Order* (Oxford: Polity, 1994) pp 2-6.

3   *Ibid*, p 6.

4   Gary Teeple, *Globalization and the Decline of Social Reform* (Toronto: Garamond Press, 1995) p 151.

5   Adolf A Berle, Jr and Gardiner C Means, *The Modern Corporation and Private Property* (New York: Macmillan, 1933); Oscar Handlin and Mary Flug Handlin, *Commonwealth: A Study of the Role of Government in the American Economy-Massachusetts 1774-1861*, revised edition (Cambridge, MA: Belknap, 1969).

6   Andrew Fraser, *The Spirit of the Laws: Republicanism and the Unfinished Project of Modernity* (Toronto: University of Toronto Press, 1990) pp 165-230.

7   Hannah Arendt, *On Revolution* (Hardmondsworth: Pelican, 1973) p 173.

8   Charter of the East India Company in Shepard B Clough, *European Economic History* (Princeton, NJ: Van Nostrand, 1965).

9   Christian Meier, *The Greek Discovery of Politics*, tr. David McLintock (Cambridge, MA: Harvard University Press, 1990).

10   Mark J Roe, 'Chaos and Evolution in Law and Economics' (1996) 109 *Harvard Law Review* 641 at p 643.

11   Mark Hager, 'Bodies Politic: The Progressive History of Organisational "Real Entity" Theory' (1989) 50 *University of Pittsburgh Law Review* 575.

12   Otto von Gierke, *Community in Historical Perspective*, ed Anthony Black (Cambridge: Cambridge University Press, 1990).

13   *Ibid*, pp 203-4.

14   *Ibid*, pp 120-2.

15   Hannah Arendt, *The Human Condition* (Chicago: University of Chicago Press, 1958).

16   Gierke, *supra* note 12 at pp 198-200.

17   Hager, *supra* note 11 at pp 650-1.

18   Harold J Laski, 'The Problem of Administrative Areas' in *The Foundations of Sovereignty and Other Essays* (London: Allen and Unwin, 1921) p 70.

19   W M Gelder, 'Legal Personality' (1911) 27 *Law Quarterly Review* 90; Harold J Laski, 'The Personality of Association' (1916) 29 *Harvard Law Review* 404.

20   Paul Hirst, ed, *The Pluralist Theory of the State* (London: Routledge, 1989).

21   Beck, *supra* note 2 at p 26.
22   Ulrich Beck, 'Freedom for Technology!' *Dissent* (Fall 1995) p 504.
23   Hannah Arendt, 'What is Authority?' in *Between Past and Future: Six Exercises in Political Thought* (New York: World, 1963) p 122.
24   *Ibid*, pp 122-3.
25   David Millon, 'Objectivity and Democracy' (1992) 67 *New York University Law Review* 1 at pp 49, 44.
26   *Ibid*, pp 37, 43, 44, 55.
27   David Millon, 'Redefining Corporate Law' (1991) 24 *Indiana Law Review* 223.
28   Alexis de Tocqueville, *Democracy in America*, tr Henry Reeves, Vol I (New York: Schocken, 1961) p 322.
29   Millon, *supra* note 25 at pp 30, 10.
30   Tocqueville, *supra* note 28 at pp 321-31.
31   *Ibid*, p 322, 325.
32   *Ibid*, p 325.
33   Andrew Fraser, 'Beyond the Charter Debate: Republicanism, Rights and Civic Virtue in the Civil Constitution of Canadian Society' (1993) 1 *Review of Constitutional Studies* 27.
34   Millon, *supra* note 25 at pp 49, 44.
35   *Ibid*, p 55.
36   Julian Franklin, 'Jean Bodin and the End of Medieval Constitutionalism' in Horst Denzer, ed, *Jean Bodin* (Munich: Beck, 1973) pp 153-66.
37   Millon, *supra* note 25 at pp 59-62.
38   Stephen Skowronek, *Building a New American State: The Expansion of National Administrative Capacities 1877-1920* (Cambridge: Cambridge University Press, 1982); Alfred A Reed, *Training for the Public Profession of the Law* (New York: Carnegie Foundation for the Advancement of Teaching, 1921) pp 89-90.
39   Wayne K Hobson, 'Symbol of the New Profession: Emergence of the Large Law Firm' in Gerard W Gawalt, *The New High Priests: Lawyers in Post-Civil War America* (Westport, CT: Greenwood, 1984) pp 3-27.
40   *Ibid*, p 9.
41   Morton J Horwitz, *The Transformation of American Law, 1870-1960: The Crisis of Legal Orthodoxy* (New York: Oxford University Press, 1992) pp 65-108.
42   *First National Bank of Boston v Bellotti* (1978) 435 US 657; *Australian Capital Television v The Commonwealth* (1992) 66 ALJR 695; *RJR-MacDonald Inc v Attorney General of Canada* (1995) 127 DLR (4th) 1.
43   Cf Hager, *supra* note 11.
44   Allan C Hutchinson, *Waiting for Coraf: A Critique of Law and Rights* (Toronto: University of Toronto Press, 1995) p 201.
45   Hager, *supra* note 11 at p 653.
46   Hutchinson, *supra* note 44 at pp 198-202.
47   Beck, *supra* note 22 at p 503.
48   *Ibid*, pp 503-7.
49   Alain de Benoist, 'End of the Left-Right Dichotomy', *Telos* 102 (Winter 1995) pp 87, 82-3, 86.
50   *Ibid*, pp 85-6.

51 Jean L Cohen and Andrew Arato, *Civil Society and Political Theory* (Cambridge MA: MIT Press, 1992) pp 57, viii-x.
52 *Ibid*, p 483.
53 *Ibid*, pp 455, 452, 470.
54 *Ibid*, pp 416-7.
55 *Ibid*, p 457.
56 *Ibid*, p 415.
57 David Gross, 'Left Melancholy', *Telos* 65 (Fall 1985) p 121.
58 Cohen and Arato, *supra* note 51 at p 483.
59 Gunther Teubner, 'Corporate Fiduciary Duties and Their Beneficiaries: A Functional Approach to the Legal Institutionalization of Corporate Responsibility' in Klaus J Hopt and Gunther Teubner, eds, *Corporate Governance and Directors' Liabilities: Legal, Economic and Sociological Analyses on Corporate Social Responsibility* (Berlin: Walter de Gruyter, 1985) p 171.
60 Paul Hirst, *Associative Democracy: New Forms of Economic and Social Governance* (Oxford: Polity, 1994) pp 55, 35.
61 Paul Hirst, *On Law and Ideology* (London: Macmillan, 1979) p 133.
62 Hirst, *supra* note 60 at pp 142, 63.
63 Cohen and Arato, *supra* note 51 at pp 482-483.
64 Hirst, *supra* note 60 at p 152.
65 Stephen M Bainbridge, 'Community and Statism: A Conservative Contractarian Critique of Progressive Corporate Law Scholarship' (1997) 82 *Cornell Law Review* 101 at pp 142, 118-119, 105-106.
66 *Ibid*, pp 135, 138.
67 Cf Robert D Putnam, *Making Democracy Work: Civic Traditions in Modern Italy* (Princeton: Princeton University Press, 1993) chapter 6.
68 Bainbridge, *supra* note 65 at pp 139-40.
69 *Ibid*, pp 145, 140, 141.
70 *Ibid*, p 145.
71 Robert Jackall, *Moral Mazes: The World of Corporate Managers* (New York: Oxford University Press, 1988) pp 195, 193.
72 *Ibid*, p 204.
73 *Ibid*, pp 193-194.
74 Bainbridge, *supra* note 65 at p 146.
75 Jackall, *supra* note 71 at p 193.
76 John Ralston Saul, *The Unconscious Civilization* (Concord, Ontario: Anansi, 1995) pp 121-122.
77 Bainbridge, *supra* note 65 at p 144.
78 *Ibid*, p 106.
79 *Ibid*, p 147.
80 Hans-Hermann Hoppe, 'The Case for Secession', *Telos* 107 (Spring 1996) p 97.
81 Bainbridge, *supra* note 65 at p 143.
82 William Blackstone, *Commentaries on the Laws of England*, Vol II (Chicago: University of Chicago Press, 1979) p 2.
83 J G A Pocock, 'Cambridge Paradigms and Scotch Philosophers: A Study of the Relations between the Civic Humanist and the Civil Jurisprudential Interpretation of

Eighteenth Century Social Thought' in Istvan Hont and Michael Ignatieff, eds, *Wealth and Virtue: The Shaping of Political Economy in the Scottish Enlightenment* (Cambridge: Cambridge University Press, 1988) p 248.

84   *Ibid*, pp 248-9.

85   Harold Perkin, *The Origins of Modern English Society 1780-1880* (London: Routledge and Kegan Paul, 1969) p 11.

86   Ged Martin, *Bunyip Aristocracy* (Sydney: Croom Helm, 1986).

87   Paul Langford, *Public Life and the Propertied Englishman 1689-1798* (Oxford: Clarendon Press, 1991).

88   Hirst, *supra* note 60 at p 146.

Epilogue:
The Rebel in *Paradise Ltd*

Summary

Democrats and populists would do well to support those few rebel capitalists ready to become the vanguard of a reflexive and responsible ruling class. We began this book with the observation that Anglo-American elites deny the existence of a ruling class. Responsibility for the survival of the common world is lodged instead in an impersonal system. Corporate law has been designed to facilitate a legalised flight from responsibility by those who nominally own the corporate system. Limited liability is only the most obvious manifestation of civic privatism within the propertied, professional and managerial classes. The abolition of property qualifications for voting and public office holding was once greeted as a triumph of democracy. It turned out that the formal abdication of the ruling class failed to prevent the emergence of the corporate sector as a distinctively modern form of benevolent despotism. The power of that corporate system has effectively deflated the sovereign authority of the liberal democratic nation state.

Since the corporate system has transcended the boundaries of the nation-state there is no reason to believe that the divine economy will not erode the spiritual foundations of Western civilisation as well. It often seems that every aspect of our being and identity now stands at risk. But the main threats now come not from nature but from a disembodied system of needs driven by the lust for money and power.

We are told by countless experts that there is nothing we can do to reverse this trend. The economy imposes strict limits on political action. If we are to believe the experts, there is certainly not much that can be done to change the nature of corporate governance. Most of those who write on the subject portray the corporation as an inherently economic entity justified by its evident utility as a device to pool and create wealth. There are those who admit that there is a problem of corporate governance created by the actual separation of ownership and control. But even they limit their prescription for reform to proposals designed to modify the behaviour of corporations in ways that either enhance or do not significantly impair their economic utility.

Nevertheless, we saw earlier that the economic interpretation of the corporate constitution could not explain the survival of the inalienable and exclusive right of shareholders to vote at general meetings and for or against members of the board of directors. Thinking of shareholder rights as merely residual makes it more rather than less difficult to explain why votes could not be bought and sold. Only political theory can answer that question. Political theory is just as relevant when one tries to understand why voting rights in corporate governance are allocated by share rather than by voice. We saw that dispersed shareholders now face formidable collective action problems that could persist even under a one person, one vote regime. Those problems could be overcome by adopting a republican model of the dual class capital structure now favoured by some major corporations. Even within the framework of existing markets for products, capital and corporate control, it is possible to carve out public spaces allowing a body of shareholders to exercise control over their joint enterprise.

The corporation is driven not just by the economic logic of efficiency but also by the political realities of power. It is no longer difficult to demonstrate that the particular forms of corporate governance now prevailing in Anglo-American societies are the products just as much of political struggles as of economic necessity. Nor is there a shortage of experts testifying to the existence of a political life internal to the business corporation. The power coalition model of the corporation now rivals the nexus of contracts theory in the contest for academic influence. The problem is that neither approach allows much scope for political action on the part of shareholders. Indeed, both those who focus on the economic utility of the corporation and those who are more interested in power coalition theory want to encourage regular and predictable patterns of corporate behaviour.

Experts mapping the political topography of corporate power evidence little interest in the political responsibility of corporate shareholders. Nor do they want to expand the capacity of shareholders to reflect upon their preferences through a political process of deliberative decision-making. Instead they explain the central role of the shareholder in corporate governance as a function of managerial dependence on the material and ideological resources available to investors. That functionalist analysis cannot account for the moral responsibility of owners to exercise care and control over the uses to which their property is put. Power coalition theory seeks only 'to provide a more complete explanation than do market theories of corporate behaviour and structure'.[1] Efforts to regulate corporate behaviour are bound to be influenced by the power model of the corporation as a coalition of stakeholder interests. This theory downgrades the role of the shareholder in the hope that managers will factor a wider range of social interests into the corporate decision-making process. But this strategy will facilitate the corporate refeudalisation of modern civil society. Who, apart from the shareholders, can claim the authority necessary to challenge and discipline the power of their managerial agents?

The constitutional choice between stakeholders and shareholders could determine the fate of modern civil society. If the law follows the path of least resistance, a multiplicity of self-aggrandising stakeholder groups will be empowered to cut deals as best they can within the corporate fiefdoms that spring up to displace or collaborate with a shrinking public sector. In this scenario, formal constitutional authority fades into irrelevance as an expanding managerial despotism finds justification in its power to produce results that show up on the bottom line. An alternative to corporate neo-feudalism is the sort of neo-federalism that could emerge from the creation of shareholder senates in the corporate sector. The stakeholder strategy rides the postmodern currents of cultural fragmentation. The neo-federal solution, by contrast, requires a sustained constitutional challenge to managerial power. Success depends upon the willingness of free citizens to act in defence of the republic.

Conclusion

Economic incentives and institutional monitoring may modify corporate behaviour. They cannot create a new civic culture of corporate governance. The republican reformation of the corporate sector will be sparked by citizens who refuse to conform to the behaviour normally expected of owners and managers. When, where and how such shareholder insurgencies will begin is obviously impossible to predict. But it is still possible to preach the gospel of reformation wherever one may happen to be. It may be, as Marxists used to say, that the objective conditions for a spontaneous spiritual awakening are ripening in the old Commonwealth countries. There is at least a chance that the hitherto unrelated problems of the republic and the economy will become tangled up one with the other in Australia and the United Kingdom, perhaps even in Canada. If so, the far-flung subjects of the British Crown could come together to reform the transnational corporate system.

We cannot look to the United States for leadership in any such movement. Long ago, the incorporation of America rendered obsolete the republican form of government enshrined in the Constitution. Efforts to resuscitate republicanism have met with public indifference. At best, the tradition remains dormant. In Australia and the United Kingdom, however, the issue of the republic has appeared on the agenda of constitutional reform. The official sponsors of the republic insist that no fundamental constitutional changes will be required to achieve their goal. But elite efforts to control the terms of the debate over republicanism appear doomed. By insisting that no fundamental constitutional change is required while warning that a failure to act will call the credibility of the nation into question, minimalists make it possible for the republic to mean anything, everything or nothing.[2] Throughout the old British Commonwealth, the republican genie has been released into a public domain subject to piecemeal takeover by the corporate sector. Who can tell what political magic it might work?

The sort of constitutional reformation that we need everywhere in the common law world will never be achieved through the captive agencies of the administrative state. Nor will any movement to civilise corporate capitalism be welcomed by those who now speak for big business. Serious and substantial debate over corporate governance has been mothballed in the universities where it poses no danger to corporate hegemony. No less supine than the much maligned passive shareholder, most academic specialists in corporate law take the lordship of capital for granted. Given the spectacular power of the contemporary corporate welfare state, it will require both moral inspiration and heroic struggle to spark and sustain an intellectual and social movement capable of carrying through the republican reformation of Anglo-American civil society. A republican reformation will have to challenge the hedonistic ethic of irresponsibility spawned by consumer capitalism. Owners of social, economic and cultural capital are now free to abdicate the responsibilities of ruling and being ruled once attached to property. For those who control the cultural and economic wealth generated by modern corporate capitalism, the satisfaction of private desires now holds more appeal than the assumption of civic responsibility. The corporate system has become a heavenly city of perpetual growth and limited liability for a vast multitude of passive investors.

This is not an altogether novel problem. Georges Sorel observed 'that the aristocracy of the old regime with its cultivation of the "art of living" had anticipated the modern cult of consumption'. Royal absolutism fostered decadence as the French aristocracy traded its 'power for the brilliant, feverish delights of the Sun King's court'. Having abandoned their civic functions, aristocrats 'no longer wanted to hear of the prudence long imposed on their fathers'. That 'escape from responsibility' became a 'dominant theme in eighteenth century aristocratic culture'. In the bourgeois age of the democratic revolution, it has been the idea of progress that has 'furnished the theoretical justification for the abrogation of reciprocal obligations, the foundation of aristocratic morality in its heroic phase, before enlightened aristocrats were corrupted by easy living'.[3] According to the bourgeois logic of collective action, every noble gesture involves a cost that the more prosaic free-rider would prefer to shift elsewhere. Indeed, the individual's unfettered right to pursue his own narrow self-interest is generally regarded as the motor of economic and social progress. French aristocrats became free-riders, much resented by the bourgeoisie who were denied a share in public authority. Nowadays, every rational economic actor wants to turn an aristocratic vice into a bourgeois virtue. Perhaps endowing the most active and energetic members of the corporate bourgeoisie with the civic functions of a senatorial elite would engender a renewed sense of *noblesse oblige*.

The moneyed and professional classes stand in need of a set of guiding beliefs about the world. The ideas inspiring a republican reformation will have to combine ethical insight and moral aspiration. It has been said that the cash value of such beliefs would 'lay in their capacity to call up unflagging devotion, to discipline resentment, and thus to change the world for the better'.[4] In opposition to the complacently bourgeois cult of progress, we must develop new forms of civic action inspired by the aristocratic ideal of heroic pessimism. The bourgeois optimist 'takes no account of the great difficulties presented by his projects' and 'frequently thinks that small reforms in the political constitution, and, above all, in the personnel of the government, will be sufficient to mitigate those evils of the contemporary world which seem so harsh to the sensitive mind'. The pessimist, on the other hand, may believe himself predestined to sin and damnation and still long for deliverance. In the 'warlike excitement which accompanies this *will-to-deliverance*,' courageous men find a satisfaction which is sufficient to keep up their spirit.[5] Corporate governance could become a constitutional matrix of civic virtue when it offers the active investor an experience amounting to the 'moral equivalent of war' at the mundane, institutional core of bourgeois civil society.[6] Shareholders with the option of transforming themselves into a senatorial elite have a powerful incentive to overcome the collective action problems facing owners in their dealings with managers and other investors.

The reform of corporate governance cannot succeed without a new sort of political theory. The corporate sector must balance conformity to the laws of economics with a *rebellious* politics that opens up new spaces for political agency and contestation. Shareholder senates would emerge as genuinely voluntary associations in the civil constitution of a modern republican society. The self-selecting membership of those governing councils would not support an attitude of mindless activism or knee-jerk opposition. The rebel who rises out of civil society to assume a position of authority 'is not someone who always says no; he or she is someone who always *can* say no; and who knows this.' Because rebellious politics 'is alive to this possibility', it 'remains tolerant and open to dissent and insurgency, offering manifold opportunities' for change in institutional structures and goals. Within the realm of corporate governance, the rebel shareholder will be bound to acknowledge his own partiality and the provisional character of his preferences. He will most likely proceed 'with caution, anticipating the opinions, objections, and even opposition of those others with whom the world is shared'.[7]

Unlike the 'democratic' concept of civil society as a junior partner to the state and the corporate sector, republican reformism incites rebellion against the managerialist norms of politics as usual. Minimalist republicanism on the Australian model is indifferent to the corporatist corruption of the bourgeois liberal republic. Since the managerial revolution, new forms of virtual representation have emerged. The systemic imperatives arising out of the global economy have become surrogates for the popular will. In eighteenth century British North America, a sovereign people set in opposition to a 'foreign' monarch could realistically pursue a programme of republicanism in one country. That is no longer possible, even for the American republic. Conversely, we can be sure that whatever happens in Australia, Canada, New Zealand or even the United Kingdom, it is only when significant numbers of American citizens join in a common movement that the republican reformation of corporate governance can finally be secured. Republicans throughout the old British dominions lying on the antipodean and northern margins of Anglo-American civilisation will have to shame the best American citizens into action, if only by force of example. By providing working prototypes of business corporations and professional associations reconstituted as civil bodies politic, we could rekindle faith in a republican tradition of civic activism long since subverted by the incorporation of the American republic into the divine economy.

Republicans in Britain and its former dominions should set out to promote a second American revolution in the realm of corporate governance. Such a movement would aim to extend the guarantee of republican government in Article IV of the American Constitution to the corporate sector. The managerial regime ushered in by the New Deal swept away the constitutional principles of limited government that had tempered the despotic potential inherent in the imperial republic of the founding generation. If it helped the federal government to regulate the national economy, even the birds and the bees would find themselves flying in interstate commerce.[8] The managerialist state has much in common with the managerialist corporation. 'Just as in the mass corporations a new elite of professional managers emerged that replaced the traditional entrepreneurial or bourgeois elite of businessmen, so in the state also a new elite of professionally trained managers or bureaucrats developed that challenged and generally became dominant over the older political elites of aristocrats and amateur politicians who occupied the formal offices of government'.[9] Both wings of the managerial elite have collaborated in the nullification of the Article IV guarantee of republican government.

For Gary Lawson, the 'post-New Deal administrative state is unconstitutional, and its validation by the legal system amounts to nothing less than a bloodless constitutional revolution'.[10] Even ardent defenders of the contemporary American corporate welfare state concede that its constitution bears little resemblance to the original design of the American republic. They may be right when they suggest that a disaster of major proportions would result from any movement to return to the original understanding of the federal constitution. It was the compelling need 'to weather the economic storms that had destroyed democracy in Europe', along with the 'transforming experience of total war' that were invoked to justify the revolution in constitutional interpretation.[11]

So long as republican government was identified with the constitutional fiction of popular sovereignty, the guarantee clause was bound to amount to little more than a dead letter. But, now that the states of the Union have been overshadowed by the growth of a vast, interlocking system of corporate governance, it makes good constitutional sense to reconstitute the public corporation as a little republic. The durability of any form of republican government worthy of the name now depends upon our capacity to institutionalise reflexive schemas of civic action within the subpolitical corporate entities straddling the heavily eroded boundary between the state and civil society. In other words, the survival of deliberative democracy requires that our understanding of the republican principles of civic freedom and political equality keeps pace with the changing institutional structure of public and private government. If governmental powers become detached from the formal constitutional structures of the federal polity and are lodged instead in ostensibly 'private' forms of corporate enterprise and professional organisation, the constitutional guarantee of republican government should follow in their wake. The original understanding of American republicanism is clearly ill-adapted to the constitutional requirements of reflexive modernisation. The question is whether the idea of the republic can be injected with fresh constitutional meaning.

In principle, the republican renaissance in Australia and the United Kingdom could provide an opportunity for ideological renovation. In practice, Australian and British republicans generally have shown little inclination to break new constitutional ground. There has been even less interest in the idea of the republic in Canada, if only because the abolition of the British monarchy would deprive the Canadian nation-state of its loyalist raison d'être. Loyalty to the Crown, not popular sovereignty, was the foundation principle of the Canadian Confederation. Canadian identity has developed through long resistance to the manifest destiny of an expansionist Yankee republic. More recently, Canada has been incorporated into the economic constitution of the Union through the North American free trade agreement (NAFTA) while retaining its nominal allegiance to the British Crown. Under these circumstances, the Canadian question posed by Goldwin Smith over a century ago demands an answer.[12] An independent Canadian republic is simply redundant. For Canadians, to become a republic is to become American. Within NAFTA, Canadians will be governed from Washington, New York and Los Angeles without being admitted to the privileges and immunities of American citizenship. The same systemic logic that dissolved the legal distinction between interstate and intra-state trade and commerce in American constitutional law will make short work of an international boundary open to the free flow of capital, technology and labour.

American policymakers want to absorb Canada within a single continental economy. Nevertheless, they will continue to treat Canadians as foreigners with no right to a voice in the government of the American republic. Formal annexation holds no attraction for Presidents, legislators and states who would have to share their political power over the management of the continental economy with well-entrenched Canadian provincial governments and their electorates. Even without annexation, the federal government in Canada could be sidelined as the provinces and business interests cut their own deals with political, economic and cultural elites south of the border.

Faced with the prospect of political obsolescence, the Canadian government could gain a new lease on life by taking the lead in a movement to provide both Canadian and American citizens with the constitutional right to participate as political equals in the corporate governance of the continental economy. Such a programme would not create a political union between Canada and the United States. Its object would be to guarantee a republican form of government in the economic constitution of North America. Even Canadian nationalists could then see in free trade an historic opportunity to press forward with Canada's civilising mission in North America.[13]

That civilising mission could begin at home with the republican reformation of the communications and culture industries. As it happens, Canadian and Australian media barons play an important role in those industries all around the world. If they shook themselves free of their simple-minded obsession with the abolition of the monarchy, republicans throughout the Commonwealth could find in their shared British roots a source of strength and inspiration. Through a common struggle to create shareholder senates in our leading media corporations, a militant, multinational British republicanism could strike a highly visible blow against the lordship of capital.

Such a movement could grow from a petty colonial rebellion within a global communications empire into a symbol of liberation for all mankind if it managed to fire the mass-mediated imagination of the American public. The loyalists of the second British empire would enjoy a sweet, posthumous revenge if Yankee republicans were finally forced to shelve the senile slogan of popular sovereignty in favour of the ancient British ideal of the mixed polity. That tantalising vision can be translated into constitutional reality only if British republicans approach the task of reform with a genuinely noble resolution, fusing a tireless optimism of the will with an unflinching pessimism of the intellect.[14] Only then will they be prepared to carry the struggle across national boundaries into the citadels of corporate power built over the historic ruins of both the American republic and the British empire.

Notes

1   Lynne L Dallas, 'Working Toward a New Paradigm' in Lawrence E Mitchell, ed, *Progressive Corporate Law* (Boulder: Westview Press, 1995) p 52.

2   Cf John Adams in Gerald Stourzh, *Alexander Hamilton and the Idea of Republican Government* (Stanford: Stanford University Press, 1970) pp 43-44.

3   Christopher Lasch, *The True and Only Heaven: Progress and Its Critics* (New York: Norton, 1991) p 307.

4   *Ibid*, p 313.

5   Georges Sorel, 'Letter to Daniel Halevy' in *Reflections on Violence*, tr. T E Hulme (New York: Huebsch, 1912) p 15.

6   Lasch, *supra* note 3 at pp 300-3.

7   Jeffrey C Isaac, *Arendt, Camus and Modern Rebellion* (New Haven: Yale University Press, 1992) pp 140-142.

8   Bruce Ackerman and David Golove, 'Is NAFTA Constitutional?' (1995) 108 *Harvard Law Review* 801 at p 857.

9   Samuel Francis, *Beautiful Losers: Essays on the Failure of American Conservatism* (Columbia: University of Missouri Press, 1993) p 97.

10   Gary Lawson, 'The Rise and Rise of the Administrative State' (1994) 107 *Harvard Law Review* 1231 at p 1231.

11   Ackerman and Golove, *supra* note 8 at p 916.

12   Goldwin Smith, *Canada and the Canadian Question* (Toronto: University of Toronto Press, 1971).

13   Cf Richard Gwyn, *Nationalism Without Walls: The Unbearable Lightness of Being Canadian* (Toronto: McClelland and Stewart, 1995) p 50.

14   Antonio Gramsci, *Selections from the Prison Notebooks*, eds, Quintin Hoare and Geoffrey Nowell Smith (New York: International, 1971) p 175.

Author Index

Subject Index